# THE CHANGEMAKER RIPPLE EFFECT

*How One Person
Can Transform the Lives
of Thousands When Driven
by Passion, Purpose
and Boldness*

Sarah Boxx

# PRAISE FOR
## *THE CHANGEMAKER RIPPLE EFFECT*

"One of my passions is helping people to fulfill their potential. In fact, I believe that the greatest gift you can give to the people you love, and those you lead, is to fulfill your potential so that you can show them how to fulfill theirs. If this book doesn't inspire you to reach deeper to achieve your full potential, I'm not sure what will. Sarah has written a compelling book that shares the stories of other real-life people to motivate us to live up to our potential and be a force for positive change in the world. Her book is one of those that will endure, impacting our world and inspiring changemakers for years to come, and I hope that includes you."
**—Hal Elrod, #1 international bestselling author of *The Miracle Morning***

"This was a very well written book. Providing personal, inspiring stories conveys the message that anyone, from any type of background has the ability to change the lives of others. Some reoccurring themes in the book were the ability of the change makers to institute change in others simply by acknowledging small gains and building each other up for more successes. The goal of this book was to share what is possible, and to encourage people to act, and this book succeeds. This inspirational, positive book was a delight to read, and provides the reader stories of other's success, and tools to begin to create positive change in their own lives and the lives of those around them, creating a ripple effect from their actions.

I found Ian Hill's story particularly touching. He is a model of how one individual can create a movement in their community and elevate it to the next level, and institute it in other areas leading to a greater benefit for even more people. Ian, along with all the other personal stories included in the book, are a great example of how always saying yes can open so many opportunities for success. Ian can find a solution in any problem, and jumps at the chance to assist in any way. He also provides a great analysis of volunteer management with regards to nonprofits, and provides a wonderful example of how to recruit and retain volunteers to work with organizations they are interested in helping. This is a useful tool for all types of people and organizations to take advantage of.

I hope this book sees the success it deserves. It is very well thought out, and has great flow. It holds the reader's attention and provides many tools for success in creating a ripple of change in their lives."
**—Kathleen Sandoval, First Lady of Nevada**

*This book is dedicated to*
*My mom, Ruthe Stanley Longaker,*
*for showing me the stars (literally),*
*supporting my dreams, introducing me to*
*irony, and believing in me always.*
*I hear your wisdom still.*


*And to*
*My best friend and husband, Sherman Boxx,*
*for your wisdom, humor, integrity,*
*generosity, and enduring love.*
*You are an amazing man.*

# TABLE OF CONTENTS

# ACKNOWLEDGMENTS

*"When you drop any new idea in the pond of the world, you get a ripple effect. You have to be aware that you will be creating a cascade of change."*
—Joel A. Barker

Like all significant accomplishments in my life, this book was not written in isolation. I would like to thank all of those who supported, encouraged, gave generously of their time, and provided their technical skills and expertise to the writing, editing and design of this book.

Thanks to all who agreed to be interviewed and become part of the story: Ian, Michelle, Cherie, Julian, Gerard and Stacey. Thank you for sharing yourself and your stories. And my gratitude also to the people whose lives you've touched who were interviewed so I could understand your impact on them: Sarah and Emily; Anne, Carol and Laura; Alan, Marian, Andrew, and Joe.

I would like to thank my JAMRAS buddies: Meg, JoAnn and Ruth Ann. Our monthly dinners and the chance to share my excitement, doubts and process with you as this was unfolding kept me fired up. You are each amazing changemakers. More than two decades of your friendship is a priceless gift.

To Amanda Rogers, thank you for helping me in the process of culling and editing content, your thoughtful suggestions, and help in finding a consistent voice. To Christian Fuenfhausen for your graphic design skills, and Candace Erynn for your photography.

Thanks to Emily Rose for being a superb coach and accountability guide throughout the process, and to the rest of the SPS Mastermind Community for support and tips along the way.

Above all, I want to thank my husband, Sherman and the rest of my family, who supported and encouraged me in writing this book, even though it took most of my limited "free" time away from them.

# INTRODUCTION

*"The effect you have on others is the most valuable currency there is."*—**Jim Carrey**

In today's world we are bombarded by negative news 24 hours a day. From local news, national news, and world news, to Facebook, Twitter, Instagram, and other social media feeds where people share their opinions and gripes; there is no escape. We have gone from a time when our news exposure was limited to our morning newspaper and coffee and maybe the odd after dinner news program, to a world where we are constantly 'plugged in' and literally unable to shut off from the outside world. At every turn, we're exposed to every type of media through laptops, computers, tablets and television, to our phones, iPods and now, watches.

Worries about our health, mental health and financial well-being (e.g. our ability to provide for basic needs and the cost of higher education), stand in the way of our good ideas and can limit our willingness to attempt change and pursue our goals or dreams that we have held for a long time. Further, whether intentional or not, family, friends, and colleagues also have the potential to cause us to doubt ourselves and our ability to achieve our personal goals.

All of this can be disheartening and overwhelming, especially for those of us who passionately believe that real change is possible. If any of this sounds like your experience, then this book is for you.

The purpose of this book is to inspire and assist you in reconnecting to a dream or passion of your own, and encourage you to "go for it." Through these stories, you will meet a variety of remarkable individuals who have achieved success and significantly improved the lives of others along the way. Each of these individuals has faced personal and professional challenges that for many others would have been a reason to quit. Yet, none of them did. You will learn about the ten characteristics they all share, and some characteristics unique to each; characteristics that we all possess or can develop in our lives.

My goal is that each person who reads this book will take from it at least one lesson or experience and be inspired to act. To know there are others who have stood in the exact spot of desire mixed with uncertainty, yet proclaimed their aspirations and stepped boldly into their own life and dreams. And, by doing that, they made a positive difference in the lives of at least 10 others whether or not they knew it at the time.

If enough of us do this—act on a dream or desire we've held, we will be able to influence the world's collective belief about life's possibilities. More and more, people will be able to see how simple it is to make a positive difference in the lives of those closest to them; and, how that difference can ripple outward to positively touch the lives of people we will never know or meet. Ultimately, you will be inspired to join hundreds of thousands of others who individually or as part of an organization are taking bold steps to follow their dreams and change the world.

In fact, one such organization who does just that is the Food Bank of Northern Nevada[1]. Their mission is to "Feed the hungry today and solve hunger tomorrow through community partnership." But it is the bigness, the boldness of their vision that moves and inspires me: HEALTHY FOOD. EVERY PERSON. EVERY DAY. This vision unites us all. It necessitates going beyond the important work of feeding those who are hungry to addressing the root causes of hunger. Achieving this vision lifts all of us up.

*"Nobody succeeds beyond his or her wildest expectations unless he or she begins with some wild expectations."*
**—Ralph Charell**

From the outset of writing this book I committed proceeds to benefit the work of the Food Bank of Northern Nevada. Even before I created the outline, identified people to interview, or figured out my way forward, I was clear that I wanted to donate the majority of the proceeds. And, because a goal is only meaningful when it's measurable and specific, I set the minimum amount I wanted to generate from sales in the first year at $50,000—enough money to help that organization make strides in addressing hunger and poverty and attract national match funding. Mind you, at the time I set the goal I had no concept of how many book sales that would require, how much time it would take to reach that target, or even what the price of either the print or electronic version of this book would be. I just knew that I would not be satisfied until sales generated at least $50,000 for the FBNN. I know they will be able to leverage these funds, partner with others and change the conditions that allow good people to move out of poverty and into stable, healthy, and hunger-free lives.

I had a dream shortly after setting this goal that I was being interviewed on national television. I was asked how it felt to have surpassed my goal by generating $100,000 in less than six months. I told the interviewer that as great as it felt, it was even better to know that so many other everyday heroes joined me in achieving it.

# CHAPTER 1
# WHO MAKES CHANGE HAPPEN?

*"Things do not change; we do."*—Henry David Thoreau

When we think about people who are making changes in the world, having an impact, it's natural to think they are somehow special or different; that they come by their success through luck, good fortune or because they knew the right people. In some respects, there are elements of truth in those assumptions.

Luck?

If luck is involved in success, its role is limited at best. The Roman philosopher Seneca pointed this out more than 2,000 years ago[2] when he said: "Luck is what happens when preparation meets opportunity."[3] People who succeed know achievement requires them to take the necessary steps; it won't be done for them.

Good fortune?

Usually people link good fortune to someone's circumstances, thinking that if they had those same conditions in their life, then they too could succeed. In truth, a person's character is a greater influence. Will they do what it takes to succeed when the going gets tough? Booker T. Washington declared that "Character, not circumstances, makes the man [person]".4 If circumstance was the sole factor for success, then Mr. Washington, who was born a slave, would never have become known as "the most influential black educator of the late 19th and early 20th centuries."5 Knowing the right people?

Absolutely. Successful people surround themselves with others who share their beliefs about what is possible, people working together to pursue excellence, people committed to learning and growing. They know and spend time with people that choose to focus on strengths—their own as well as others'—and opportunities even in times of adversity, rather than giving their power over to barriers and obstacles. And, successful people know and spend time with others that consciously choose each day to become more of the person they want to be.

## WHO YOU WILL MEET

In this book, you will read stories of six very different individuals, each in different stages of life. Each has overcome challenges to achieve personal goals and dreams. You will learn what motivates and influences each individual when times are challenging. You will also read stories of the changes in the lives of the people they've touched: the "ripple effect" of their actions.

You will meet Ian, a businessman and entrepreneur, who for the past 25 years devoted his life to volunteering and improving the conditions and resources for children and youth. His work has spanned multiple continents and he has been a board member, organization founder, motivational speaker, trainer, coach, fund raiser, community champion, and a volunteer recruiter. Ian has faced personal hardships and encountered heartbreaking situations, but he has never stopped; he has grown and changed over the years and shares some of the key lessons he's learned along the way. As part of Ian's story, you will also meet Sarah and Emily; a mother and daughter who have both benefited from, and been inspired by Ian and his work. In their own way, they are both pursuing their dreams and making the world a better place.

Then, there's Julian. The main constant in Julian's life has always been music. It was there for him when he was being victimized at school for being poor and smart—a target for bullies. It was there for him when he was suicidal and chose instead to travel the United States. And, he took his music with him when he began working in carnivals at the age of 18. Music remains Julian's constant today. In addition to working long, physically demanding days in construction, he challenged the Guinness World Record in order to build the music community and grow the economic viability the local music scene in Chico, California.

Michelle is someone that has touched the lives of people around the world through her professional and athletic endeavors. Her zest for life and her belief that each person can achieve their goals if they take it one step at a time has inspired people to reach beyond what they thought possible. Michelle learned from a young age how fragile life can be. She has seen firsthand how easily a young person's life can be dismissed, cast aside and even lost when the world they live in is at odds with what is expected. She has felt the frustration when adults and systems don't take into consideration the unique situations of each child, but instead try to squeeze them to fit into the system. It is no wonder that she has committed to encouraging and building people up in her various roles as a sibling, student, athlete and professional business woman. You will hear stories of how Michelle's commitment to train and grow in her own life has influenced the lives of others, including me.

Next, you will meet Gerard and Stacey. Coming from very different backgrounds and two different countries, each has faced their own unique challenges. Gerard grew up in France and is now an award winning documentary film maker. With Clint Eastwood as one of his role models, he found his life totally transformed when he had a vision of his death while serving in the military. He embarked on a new path to expose the horrors of war and backroom deals and profiteering, which eventually brought him to the United States, where he met Stacey. Stacey grew up in beautiful Northern California with her own story of change and transformation. Influenced by social injustice at an early age, she was determined to make a difference. Many years and detours later she met Gerard and they went in a new direction. Already reaching thousands of youth and adults with their teaching, they continue to learn and advance their work, even as they continue to face obstacles. Today, Gerard and Stacey are early in the journey of bringing hope, and sharing their courage and real stories of pioneers and "everyday heroes" so more can be inspired to act.

Finally, you will meet Cherie. Cherie had a very fortunate childhood and had a special bond with her father. Later in life however, she faced some definite hardships and challenges that ultimately led her to Canada, then west to Reno, Nevada where she lives today. In her role as President and CEO of the Food Bank of Northern Nevada (FBNN), where in fact the majority of profits from book sales will be donated, Cherie championed thoughtful discourse, bold actions and advocacy to change the image and role of food banks in Nevada. She built a supportive network of changemakers and together they grew the FBNN from a small nonprofit to the massive success it is today; all of which required stretching and growing, working through challenges and personal loss, and sustaining her belief that ending hunger is indeed possible.

# CHAPTER 2
# IT STARTS CLOSE TO HOME AND GROWS FROM THERE

*"Think twice before you speak, because your words and influence will plant the seed of either success or failure in the mind of another."*—**Napoleon Hill**

Do you believe there are heroes among us? Not superheroes, but everyday people who live next door to you and me. People who go about their daily lives much the same as everyone else, with one difference: they are driven by purpose; a goal or vision that propels them forward in spite of the obstacles they face. Simply because they stood up and chose to listen to their inner voice, take action, follow their dream, or champion someone else, they change the lives of several others for the better.

I know there are heroes among us. I have proof. Many of them have touched my life in profound ways. Some of these people I know personally, and others I know from a distance. Regardless, each has in some way shown me, taught me, or influenced me to stretch beyond what I thought possible; to reach beyond my current grasp for something that truly matters to me. And, to step out of my comfort zone in order to help and improve conditions for others.

My mom Ruthe was one of those people. She greatly influenced what I thought was possible. From a very early age I remember her encouraging and supporting my expression and exploration. When I was in fifth grade, I wanted to be an artist and I had a desire to paint a mural—in our house. My mom gave me a canvas of a different type; all of the kitchen cabinets were mine to paint. She never asked what I was going to paint, and I didn't share any sketches or ideas ahead of time. She only asked that I clean up after myself. For the longest time, our white metal cabinets remained adorned with the designs I painstakingly painted; I think they were even still there when I left home to live on my own.

My dad traveled a lot when we were young. That meant my mom set the tone for how we were raised, and more often than not, my dad agreed. Growing up, we always had at least one dog and one cat. However, at various times we had snakes, pigeons, hamsters, chicks, a duck, and a raccoon. This might sound reasonable if we lived in the countryside, but we lived in quiet neighborhood, on a residential street, with a conservatively sized backyard. So, why not one more animal?

Like many young girls, I wanted a horse. I loved horses and one of my best friends rode. I told my parents that I wanted a horse and asked if they would buy one for me; I thought this was a reasonable request. Obviously, I had no concept of what a horse would cost or how much care it would require. I had not considered that if I got a horse, then my younger sister and brother would also want their own.

While my parents were barely getting by and providing for our large family, that kind of cash outlay and monthly obligations were not in our immediate future. They gave me the 11-year old's version of the explanation: "No. We can't afford to buy a horse for you right now. Then there's your sister and brother to think about, too. And, there's more than just the purchase cost. You will have monthly boarding costs, plus regular shoeing and vet bills, too."

This is what I heard:

"No . . . not now. We can't afford to buy a horse for you."

Perfect. It wasn't a clear or firm "No, you can't have a horse." This problem had a solution. They couldn't *afford to buy the horse*. I just needed to earn the money to buy a horse so they wouldn't have to.

I countered, "What if I had enough money to buy a horse on my own?

Would you be willing to help with the boarding?"

Evidently, that seemed more reasonable; or, perhaps they figured by the time I earned that amount of money I'd be a lot older (or maybe even lose interest). Either way, they said every kid's favorite response,

"We'll think about it." In my family, that meant the door of opportunity remained open a crack. I understood it would now be up to me to convince them it was a good idea; and, to show them I was serious.

I set my sights on earning $500 dollars. I didn't know if that would be enough, but I figured it would be close. I divided it by the number of hours I would need to babysit at $0.50/hour and realized that wasn't going to work out, especially since I really disliked babysitting as a means of earning money. So, I set out on a different path that led me to my first job bottling saddle soap, now at the age of 12. When I ended the school day I walked to the saddle shop where I worked until dinner. My mom supported me, just as long as my grades didn't suffer—no matter that I was underage! I was excited to be doing something to achieve a goal. When I had questions about how to handle certain situations, she offered guidance.

Eventually, I earned enough money to buy my first horse; and it hadn't taken as long as I thought! Then it came time to negotiate ongoing costs for upkeep and care. My parents helped with monthly boarding; and, other costs such as shoeing, vet bills, etc. were my responsibility.

Their decision to remain open to seeing what I could do, and my mom's ongoing encouragement to work toward what I wanted even if they could not help me financially, taught me valuable lessons:

"No" just means "not yet."

Saying "we'll see" or "let's think about it" leaves the door of opportunity open for someone that has a dream and the ambition to pursue it.

You don't need to have everything figured out before beginning to move forward. Just start.

Keeping your "eye on the prize" goes a long way, when what you want seems a long way off.

I am capable of doing, having or achieving something that matters to me as long as I take ownership and don't wait for permission or for someone else to do it for me.

I'm certain there were times I shared my dreams or goals with my mom and she secretly wished that I would change my mind or go in a different direction, but, she never conveyed her worries or doubts to me. And if others did, she told me to ignore them. As a result, I figured I could accomplish anything I wanted to do; I could go anywhere, do anything—if I cared enough. I didn't have to be perfect, but I did have to start. If it didn't work out, it would not be the end of the world. But, if I never tried, I would never know what I could have accomplished.

## ADMIRAL MCRAVEN'S CHALLENGE

When I was conducting research for this book, I came across an article about the 2014 Commencement speech delivered by Naval Adm. William H. McRaven (Ret. ninth commander of U.S. Special Operations Command). When I read the speech I was amazed at the simplicity and magnitude of impact that happens when someone starts off and continues through each day, by: doing the little things right; getting and giving help along the way; measuring others only by the size of their heart; continuing through adversity and relying on inner strength; being willing to fail; recognizing and living with the power of hope; and, never quitting.

I agree with the bold challenge he made as he stood before the University of Texas at Austin's graduating class. He asserted that if these 8,000 graduates would commit to positively changing the lives of just 10 individuals, and those 10 people did the same for 10 more people, then within only 5 generations, the lives of 800 million people will have been changed for the better.

Think about it. That is more than TWO TIMES the current US population, or the combined US and European Union populations. All that change would be possible if only one graduating class—or 8,000 people—decided to be intentional in making a positive change that could ripple outward with its effects.

Admiral McRaven shared stories of how easily a person's life can be changed in an instant, and how that change then ripples outward to affect generations. He talked about how one commander's decision to go a particular direction, thereby avoiding a close-in ambush, saved the lives of 10 soldiers. He told of how more than a dozen soldiers lived because an officer trusted her gut that something felt off, and changed direction in response; narrowly missing a 500-pound IED. Those two officers' decisions resulted in 22 soldiers surviving; and so too, did future generations of those soldiers' children's children.

Amazing.

I share Admiral McRaven's viewpoint, that just one person can make a difference. I've seen it happen in my life where the words, encouragement, offers of support (or even the absence of negativity) helped me—and others like me—to recognize opportunities and take chances we might never have done otherwise. Because of what just one person does, someone else's life is changed. I call this the *Changemaker Ripple Effect.*

Certainly other factors are at play, but if you keep it simple and focus on the potential impact that one decision for the ultimate 'good' can have, you can see how easily future generations can be affected by one solitary individual's efforts.

Admiral McRaven told the graduating class that anyone can change the world, from anywhere.

The real question is:

*What will the world look like **after** you change it?*

Like Admiral McRaven pointed out, one decision—in the case of my parents, it was the decision to say "maybe" instead of "no" when I wanted a horse—set me on a lifelong path of trusting my ability to pursue my goals. That lesson led me to decide that "no" to something I'm passionate about, only means "not yet" if I care enough to take action. Finally, by saying or doing something thoughtful or encouraging in everyday situations, we can have unimagined influence for good in the world.

I have thought many times over how grateful I am that my parents did not have the means to buy me that horse. If they had, they would have robbed me of experiencing the exhilaration of achievement and self-reliance. It's also likely that I would not have been as willing to attempt solutions to other challenges, or trusted in my ability to do something I did not (currently) have the skills or knowledge to do.

My mom died in April of 1996. Even though it's been 20 years, I remember that day as if it was yesterday. To this day, I experience her influence and hear her words of wisdom, encouragement and belief in my ability. That gift of a lifetime (literally) has no price.

# CHAPTER 3
# IAN HILL

## INTRODUCTION

I met Ian Hill nearly 20 years ago. At the time, all I knew about Ian was that he was a local businessman and entrepreneur who wanted to make things right for children. Ian sees a problem and immediately wants to fix it. He has no patience for obstacles or for working through processes that are slow or ineffective. He is not someone that just identifies problems and complains, expecting someone else to do something about it. Ian is a man who finds a solution, rolls up his sleeves and commits his time, energy and heart to making a difference. In short, Ian is living proof to others of what is possible—when a single individual makes a commitment to make a difference. That is what he was doing when our paths first crossed.

I can honestly say that Ian changed my concept of what is possible by reminding me, as he reminds others, that while we may be only one individual, we can make a difference. We must act in full faith of that belief. It is clear to me that over the past two decades, Ian's passion and commitment had continued to burn bright. It wasn't until I spent time talking with Ian that I learned just how many people's lives he has influenced on different continents, and what he learned about himself in the process.

## THE 4TH STREET CONNECTION—FROM KIDS KORNER TO LET THEM BE KIDS (LTBK)

*"Action is the foundational key to all success."*
**—Pablo Picasso**

Ian is a man who has always been passionate about helping young people in need. He deeply felt that more should be done to help kids. He was determined and willing to build community support to do the work to make a difference. And that's just what he did. Ian learned a lot from people working on the front lines. One of those people was Jack—a friend of Ian's who was a Sergeant with the Reno Police Department.

At the time (mid-1990s), Jack was part of a huge community collaboration called Kids Korner. One of the Kids Korner activities was "knock and talks" up and down Reno's 4th Street corridor—a part of town known for its weekly motels, street walkers, low incomes and poverty. During these walks they visited residents of the two dozen area motels. The purpose was to reach out to low income, disadvantaged and "at-risk" families. They wanted to learn the specific needs of very young children (birth to six) and their families living in this area. These were people who were often the most underserved because they were invisible to the network of services available once a child enters the school system.

As Ian tells it, Jack was doing "door knocks" and finding all these kids who had significant problems, issues and challenges. Ian wanted to join with the other organizations that were trying to help, but Ian was frustrated with the situation. He just wanted to help the kids.

Ian considered the significant benefits of a fund that these service providers could easily access for things to make these kids just feel like kids, such as for: birthday cakes, shoes, and sports equipment.

This inspired Ian to be the one to create a fund just for that.

You see, Ian was regularly asked to deliver paid motivational speeches as a result of his perseverance in the face of adversity; and, this fund is exactly where he wanted to invest his honorariums.

His motivations were personal. Ian's life had a very rough beginning to say the least. He had been adopted and smuggled out of Iran and brought to the United States as a baby. He was given to people his parents met at a cocktail party. They raised him in the U.S. under grueling circumstances. People told him he was "worthless, a piece of crap." He knows first-hand what that does to a person's self-esteem and how badly it feels. This gave him an appreciation of those who go without, who live in the shadows, or who have been told similar lies about their worth.

Although people who see him on stage giving a key note speech might not be able to tell the road had often been bumpy for Ian. Youth that interact with him in classrooms may not know his life story. Young boys and girls he coaches in community soccer leagues may have no clue whatsoever that there had been many times that Ian could have given up on his dream; times where many others would have quit or at least backed down, scaled back their vision of what is possible and settled for less.

But, Ian was determined to impact these children and youth in a positive way through his speeches; in more ways than one. For Ian the answer seemed clear. He would use the money that he received from his motivational speeches to create a fund to just *let them be kids*. And, that was the beginning of the *Let Them Be Kids* (LTBK) initiative in Reno. Ian needed to partner with a nonprofit organization whose mission aligned with his own to be a fiscal agent and manage the money. The Children's Cabinet, Inc. became that organization. Within one year Ian donated between $11,000 and $12,000 just from his speeches alone. Since Ian was not a particularly wealthy man, this was quite an accomplishment!

That first year had its own ripple effect.

## LTBK RENO—INVOLVING OTHERS TO INCREASE SUCCESS

*"It's stunning to me what kind of an impact even one person can have if they have the right passion, perspective and are able to align the interest of a great team."*
—Steve Case

After a short while, the news of the LTBK initiative grew. Donating his speech money endeared Ian to a lot of people. That had not been his goal; but, because he was giving his money away people started reaching out to him. Ian's passion led to others wanting to be involved. It led to others wanting to access services and supports. As a result, more funding was needed.

The first LTBK fund raising event took place. In one night, more than $10,000 was raised. After that, more people started getting involved and the work of LTBK expanded to reach even more kids; kids in need who were living in other areas of the community. One Christmas, Ian, LTBK and partners were able to put twelve hundred pairs of shoes on kids' feet by working together.

*Let Them Be Kids* is also how Ian met his wife: "The first time I met my wife Gina, it was because she asked me for a donation". She asked him for $1,500 for a youth dance outreach program.[6] Gina appreciated the power that dance could have in a young person's life. As a child she danced all the time. She danced in restaurants and on commercials. It gave her a foundation that took her around the world. Extending that chance to youth seemed only natural to Gina so she sought the aid of LTBK.

Then LTBK rolled onto the next project, an ESL (English as a second language) program called *I Can Do Anything*. Thousands of English language learners whose children attended local schools participated in the free classes; classes taught by volunteers. It was a program championed by Ed Heywood, an amazing elementary school principal with a history of community involvement, in order to benefit his students' long term success.

*I Can Do Anything* is what Ian believes is possible when people care enough to take action. This belief statement went on to become the name for the first charter school in Nevada. He worked with his wife to establish a performing arts high school, as a part of *I Can Do Anything*. And, he had spearheaded the effort to establish the Bailey Charter Elementary School that serves kindergarten through sixth grade students. All of those efforts fed and built on each other.

## LTBK—A CONTINENT AWAY

*"Collaboration is the best way to work. It's the only way to work, really."*—**Antony Starr**

In 2013, Let Them Be Kids extended their reach to positively impact the lives of school kids in the Ho

Municipality of Ghana, a small community in a time zone eight hours ahead of Carson City, Nevada and 7,500 miles away. They helped build classrooms for the Anyirawase L.A. Primary School; an important contribution to education by anyone's standards. Yet, even with the new classrooms, more needed to be done to have the kind of impact the group wanted.

The school still needed teaching tools to help their students succeed. They needed to address the barrier of ongoing, recurring costs for science labs and text books. Both of these items needed constant updating to reflect changing knowledge and understanding in science.

Enter a collaborative solution: *Let Them Be Kids* teamed up with high school senior, Porfirio Jauregui from Carson City, Nevada. The goal? To send the school solar powered generators and laptops. They would also provide a satellite connected Internet receiver that would link the school to the latest information and emerging research. Short term gains meant that the kids would have good information and were able to learn. Longer term gains were additional career opportunities because of the Internet and computer capabilities. High demand technology career paths would become accessible, such as software engineer, systems analyst, and network security specialist, along with a host of other online study options.

Another community partner in Carson City, *Comma Coffee*, stepped up to help. They offered space for volunteers to check the donated computers, remove any viruses, install anti-virus software, and make them run efficiently. In the process, anyone interested in the basics of using a computer and the Internet would gain knowledge and skills.

Why was this project so important for *Let Them Be Kids* to support? What inspired them to help a school so far away? Simple: it fit their mission to help build stronger communities across the world and to help bring fun, play, and education to all children and families.

And for Ian, it was another chance to find a solution to a problem that should not exist in the first place.


## ADVERSITY AND CHANGE: BECOMING A COMMUNITY BUILDER

*"When life knocks you down, try to land on your back. Because if you can look up, you can get up. Let your reason get you back up."*—**Les Brown**

While Ian was succeeding in his community work, other areas of his life were falling apart. In fact, he reached a point where he felt he had destroyed his life. He knew how to create success for others; he had dedicated his heart and time to making those things happen. He knew how to generate revenue and support for nonprofits and charities far better than for his own enterprises. His devotion and focus to the causes that meant so much to him absorbed his energy and focus. Ultimately, it exacted its toll on Ian. His personal business ventures failed. His marriage faltered. Everything was falling apart. His friends, or people he had considered to be friends, left him; or more politely, just turned their backs on him when he needed them the most. There was no particular reason to remain in Reno and continue doing the same things, while expecting to get different results.

Ian needed to make a change in both location and direction. He wanted to rebuild his life so he moved his family to Canada. "Canada embraced me. Canada loved me. Canada held me. Canada nurtured me. Canada accepted me."

It was like the early days in Reno, when he was just beginning his speaking and philanthropic work. He had felt loved and accepted in Reno, and so he gave back. He experienced a similar feeling in Canada, and so he gave his all to Canada.

He gave his time and finances, even when he and his family had nothing. That defined who he was. He was moved and inspired by seeing possibilities and doing what had not been done before in communities across Canada.

After much thought and reflection, Ian and his family created an online program called *Becoming a*

*Community Builder*[7]; a leadership development program to grow leadership one person at a time. After pilot testing, the program was launched to small, rural communities across Alberta, Canada in September 2014. The program focuses on creating behavioral change through "The Change Continuum." This is a blended learning model, combining: live-streaming video and coaching; reinforcement exercises and motivational emails; and, access to on-demand video through a learning portal. The goal is to support performance improvement for youth and adults.

"The key to building a thriving community today is community leadership capacity." Ian believes that it takes each one of us to change the world—to build and improve communities; our communities. It takes personal and community leadership excellence from formal and informal leaders in every sector or "silo" from every corner of the community: "It's the informal leadership capacity. It's the people without the titles that make the difference in a community; the people closest to the problem are the ones to solve the problem. It's all about leadership."

Ian's ambitious goal was to build community leadership. What happened? The program prompted the selection of 15 Lighthouse Regions in Rural Alberta with participation by over 2,200 citizens—from every walk of life, 40% of whom were "not the usual suspects" or formal leaders. They came from communities, municipalities and counties across Alberta, including Parkland County; County Two Hills; County Ponoka; Regional Municipality of Wood Buffalo, Grande Prairie, Vermilion, Bonnyville, Cold Lake, Stony Plain, Delburne, Nanton, Hanna, Consort and other rural communities to gain leadership skills through training generally targeted to larger communities.

Did it make a difference? Did it ripple out? YES.

One person decided to take what they learned through Becoming a Community Builder and run for school board. That one decision affected that person's life, set an example for all those they know and whose lives they touch, and, ultimately for the community they stepped up to serve.

And, the *Becoming a Community Builder* website has become a "go-to" for many of the provincial governments when it comes to Canadian capacity building.[8]

"Today, 80% of all rural Albertans have gone through the *Becoming a Community Builder* program. That means, in rural Alberta, one thousand regular citizens and informal leaders, completed the training program for free. The only commitment that they had to make was that they'd go out and try to make their community a better place to live."

Since taking stock, Ian and his team have been doing projects all across Canada. They focus on kids and communities, just like in Reno—but now it's for an entire country.


## LET THEM BE KIDS CANADA

*"Far and away the best prize that life has to offer is the chance to work hard at work worth doing."*
—**Theodore Roosevelt**

In his professional community development work, Ian places a strong emphasis on engaging in hands-on grassroots efforts as a catalyst for broader social change. This perspective is directly informed by his own, on-the-ground efforts as founder and Volunteer Chairman of *Let Them Be Kids Canada*, a Canada-wide not-for-profit organization. *Let Them Be Kids Canada* (LTBK) had its roots in the *Let Them Be Kids* work Ian started in Reno, Nevada a decade earlier. Ian credits those who stepped up and said, "Yes" we believe you can, and "Yes," we will support you in any way we can. Hearing those words is all it took for him to take off on his path to change the world.

Through *Let Them Be Kids Canada*, Ian and his team raised funds and volunteer support to build playgrounds, skate parks and fitness parks in areas of need. Through *Let Them Be Kids*, Ian has seen firsthand the powerful impact of a common goal—how a shared project can inspire increased community capacity, resilience and pride.

One LTBK project was community-built playgrounds conducted as a community capacity building exercise. The approach relied on the community and used the skills, talents and assets already present. The playground builds were very successful. After the first ten or twelve had been completed, Kool-Aid[9] contacted Ian to say they would like to be the LTBK corporate sponsor across Canada.

"It was amazing. How does that happen? The next thing we know, we had completed 168 playgrounds and a movie was made about the initiative."

## SUCCESS IS NOT A ONE-PERSON SHOW— VOLUNTEERS

*"Remember that the happiest people are not those getting more, but those giving more."*
—**H. Jackson Brown, Jr.**

No one can achieve big impact on their own. It takes others, and depending on the size of the effort, it can take many others. For some people this is where they hit a brick wall. Some push through. Others turn back. Others, like Ian, build a team of champions over time.

The nature of community involvement or volunteerism has changed.

Ian talks about the changes and how he's adapted to be successful:

"In the past it was obligatory to volunteer, to contribute. You had to participate because you could die if you didn't participate [in civic society]. Then along the way we became a more sophisticated society. An individual's participation in the community or in 'giving back' became 'prove it to me.' In other words, prove to me that this [my contribution] is going to be good for me. "It's become more of a 'what's in it for me?' mentality when it comes to participating."

Conversely, organizations would say, "Come and help us, come and help us! Come and help us, come and help us!" People respond and then organizations say, "Now let us tell you exactly what we need you to do."

When it comes to volunteers, Ian has had great success. His approach is simple: just ask people to participate in whatever manner they are comfortable. The more important question in Ian's mind is this: what can organizations do to make it easier for the volunteers they seek to participate and know they are valued and welcomed? What can they do to help volunteers create their own experience?

"It's not the volunteer's responsibility to make the relationship work." Ian believes that the reason people don't volunteer is because many volunteer-based organizations, community-based organizations and nonprofits don't understand today's citizen and how to create the environment to allow them to participate. If organizations started from a place of being of service to their prospective volunteers, they would have better results. If organizations started from that place, people would be more comfortable volunteering and they would do it more often.

Ian has applied this philosophy to his own work by asking some simple questions of prospective volunteers based on what will be meaningful for them and what they really want out of the experience. Then, Ian and his organization gauges the volunteer's desire and fit between that person and the organization. If so, the next step is to create those experiences for the volunteer. "You do that and that person comes back! And they're going to come back over and over and over again."

Ian lets volunteers "carve" their own experience to whatever degree possible. That's the caveat, that's the parenthetic add-on: *to whatever degree possible.* Sometimes there isn't a fit between what the volunteer wants and what the organization can offer. When this happens, it's good to know early on, so the volunteer can be redirected to an organization or volunteer opportunity that more closely meets their needs. That allows the organization to focus on the volunteers that really are a match.

So, if a non-profit, community organization or other group would create a place, or change a service so that volunteers (users) could create their own experiences, they (the organizations) would see volunteers engaged and returning to help over and over. "When we treat volunteers as customers and focus on high quality customer service, we get better results and everyone's experience is better."

And this is exactly what *Let Them Be Kids* in Canada did. When they started the Playground Project they set up a website[10] that allowed "hundreds upon hundreds of volunteers to come out and create their own experience. We asked them what time they wanted to come to help build the playground. We asked them what they wanted to do. We asked them how long they'd like to do it . . . they told us and we let them do it."

## FROM CANADA TO COACH HILL

Even though Ian was very successful in Canada, he had done all he needed to do and it was time for he and his family to move back to Carson City. They had roots there and it was only time before a return made the most sense.

Ian's daughter began to show an interest in playing soccer and had signed up with the local recreation league for the American Youth Soccer Organization

(AYSO). The AYSO was a volunteer-driven youth soccer program for kids; and, continuing his beliefs about the volunteer experience, in true Ian form, he became a volunteer coach that first year—Coach Hill. Everything Ian learned over the years, including how to successfully engage community, volunteers and youth came into play upon his return to Carson City. This included finding ways to build and support youth leadership in whatever forum made sense for youth, including soccer.

## A RIPPLE EFFECT: SARAH AND EMILY

Ian's work with youth soccer, and specifically youth in Carson City, Nevada directly touched the lives of a family I know—a friend and colleague, Sarah.

Sarah's daughter Emily had also signed up to play soccer that year. It was her first time ever playing soccer.

Just before the first practice of the season, Coach Hill called Emily's parents and invited them to come to his pre-league parents' meeting. That was their first interaction with Coach Ian Hill. Already, this recreation league seemed different.

He wanted to make sure they understood everything they needed to as a league parents. Sarah had no idea what to expect. Ian began by going over his coaching philosophy and the high expectations he has for himself. He shared his expectations for the kids and parents as well, but the focus was more on what he would do.

Powerful. Coach Hill leaves an impression.

That year there were lots of teams, and lots of volunteer coaches. Throughout that first Fall season, Sarah watched him coach the team of girls. They won some games, they lost some games, but they learned so much more. At the end of that season, they were city champions. That was a really big deal, since Emily wasn't the only first-time soccer player on the team.


## EXPANDING REACH — GROWING FROM ONE SOCCER TEAM TO THREE

During the spring soccer season, many of the same players and families were together once again. And, once again the girls were successful. After that, the parents began throwing around the idea of having the girls stay together, on a club team.

One parent in particular, Rowena, was very active and engaged. Sarah remembers Coach's response being something like, "If we're going to do this, it's going to be for everyone. It's not just going to be for our kids, kids who have access. It's going to be for everybody in Carson City that needs and wants to play."

Coach understood that the overarching barrier for many kids and their families is the financial cost of participation. There are also clusters of neighborhoods where there is not real access to sports, either because of cost or travel barriers. Coach Hill saw that need from the beginning and declared, "That's the team we're going to have. We're going to make sure it's open and accessible to everyone. We'll have good coaching and really good teams."

Sarah recounts that it was Ian and Rowena that really led the effort and then looked to others' engagement to make it happen. They turned to the founding members of the current team, parents and families who wanted to be a part of it going forward. Those were people who were willing to do what it takes to get a club started. "We were one of those families who stepped up and said, 'Yeah, we want to be a part of this. We'll do what it takes to help.'"

The club started its tryouts. A few kids came out for each one. At first it seemed like it may only be one team. Then an amazing thing began happening. New people showed up to try out. These were the kids who really *needed* to be there, to be a part of something big. One of the first of the new group of youth to try out was a little older, maybe 14 or 15. She came with another girl. They were too old to play on the younger girls' team, and there wasn't enough to form a high school team. Then, all of a sudden, there was a group of high school girls, some of them, again who had never played, some of them who had played, but who were there wanting to be coached and wanting to be part of this league. It completely changed the dynamics of the league.

There were other considerations for expanding the league. Each age group has to be structured carefully to adhere to league rules. There were additional expenses and league fees; and, not all parents were in a position to pay the fees. Then there was the question of location. There wasn't actually a field for these girls to use, as the main soccer field in Carson City wasn't available.

Coach was not deterred. "Yes" became the answer to everything. "Yes, we can make it work. Yes, we're going to make it happen. Yes, we'll figure it out. Yes, we'll come up with the money. Yes, it's going to be there."

So everyone just kept running aggressively toward that goal of making things happen so all girls could play. The vision and goals were clear. Coach considered obstacles as problems waiting for solutions. He found the solution and continued onward. He was unwavering. Nothing was going to stand in the way.

Then it happened: all of the girls were playing soccer.

This astounded Sarah. "If you had asked me [in the beginning] if we would have 60 girls playing soccer, I would have said, 'No way. This is Carson City. We're just getting started. We'll be lucky to have one team.'" "If you had asked if we could figure out how to pay the fees for 75% of those kids to play soccer, I would have said, 'Maybe. If we had more time, certainly.' But I never would have thought that in such a short amount of time we could have accomplished all of it together."

Stopping or quitting never entered the field of possibilities. It was all about finding a workaround to the challenges. When the online registration process didn't work as planned, the parents did a workaround; they simply entered people's information for them. Financially, they just kept asking for money.

"Again, it was Ian's raw, driving force and commitment to the success of this work that moved us forward when things really got sticky." In the end it all worked out.

## THE NEXT AUDACIOUS GOAL— INTERNATIONAL SOCCER

*"Follow your passion, be prepared to work hard and sacrifice, and, above all, don't let anyone limit your dreams."*—**Donovan Bailey**

Another goal Ian had in mind was to take the kids to Canada to watch the Women's World Cup Soccer finals. It would be an amazing experience and one he wanted *all* the kids to have.

He asked the parents, "Wouldn't it be amazing to have our young women go and play internationally? It would build their confidence. It would be an incredible experience. This is going to happen."

Sarah remembers looking at him and thinking that there was just no way. It just seemed so unbelievable. They were still trying to pay the league fees for all the kids. They were managing online registrations for people. They were trying to deal with all the operational challenges of getting things going at a time when not all families were able to be engaged in the regular league activities. How would they ever manage to raise enough money to get all of the kids and parents to Canada?

Yet, they did. Ian and nearly 100 people—youth soccer players and their parents and volunteers from Carson City, Nevada—had crossed the border to watch the Women's World Cup finals. They had raised $75,000 in 75 days; all because of Ian's audacious goal and the passion, purpose and boldness of parents and community volunteers. That trip produced some unexpected gifts along the way.

# AN UNEXPECTED GIFT (CHANGING PERCEPTIONS)

*"It's not what you look at that matters, it's what you see."*—**Henry David Thoreau**

There were mostly young girls and their families who traveled from Carson City to Canada for the World Cup. But there was also a group of high school boys. They had a really good team; in fact, Sarah considered it an amazing team. Since Sarah had spent most of her time with the girls' soccer club, she did not really know the boys' team members. She was not as comfortable with them as she was with the girls on the club. The boys were older, and less connected to the parents. They were their own pack. In fact, there was one boy who even seemed a little intimidating to Sarah. The trip to Canada had stops along the way where the Carson youth could meet kids from Canadian counterparts. One stop was at a high school in Macomb, Canada. Students from that school were hosting the Carson youth. They were sharing a little bit about their lives in Canada. Then they asked some of the kids from Carson to share. It wasn't planned or scripted. One of the youth who spoke was the young, tough, 'intimidating' soccer player. His story painted a much different picture of him than his outward appearance.

He described how his life had been really great in the beginning. His parents had come to the U.S. from Mexico. Then it turned difficult. He didn't provide details beyond saying that he and his entire family had been sent back to Mexico. Other hardships followed. At a certain point, he made a choice to come back to the United States and continue his education. This decision meant he would be separated across a border from his family. He wouldn't even have someone to live with when he came back. But he came anyway. He made the tough choice and saw it through.

He went on to share his perspective on family with the American and Canadian kids: "I get really frustrated when people are angry with their parents or when they say bad things about their parents. I haven't even seen my parents in years. And, they've never seen me or watched me play a soccer game." It was a brave and personal thing to share with so many strangers.

After that day, two really amazing things happened. Both were unexpected ripple effects of the trip to Canada and this young man's decision to share his story. First, a stranger in the audience volunteered money for this young man to travel home to Mexico and visit his family. The second thing was that Sarah saw this boy for who he really was, rather than what she originally assumed him to be. That was a pivotal moment for Sarah, as she explains:

"The days on the road were long. We would get home at these ridiculously late times after playing soccer or being at an event. Often it was midnight or later following a day of driving and playing soccer." In addition to Emily, Sarah was traveling with her young son Johnny. He'd been asleep for the past 2 hours of their trip. When they stopped for the night she had luggage and other things to carry, in addition to her sleeping child. She needed to get Johnny settled into bed. Then, she had meetings to attend.

"So we pulled into the hotel. I've got Johnny falling all over me. I've got luggage. Then Coach asks somebody to help me." The person that stepped up to help was the same young man who spoke about family and being apart from them. The kid who just moments prior, had seemed a little intimidating to Sarah.

"He picked up Johnny and he carried him up [to the room], and he put him to bed. I thought that was such an amazing thing to see and experience: this kid who I never would have known in any other situation or circumstance . . . I never would have thought he would be the one carefully carrying my son upstairs and putting him to bed. He just really stepped up as a leader that day. Again I think it was because he was inspired to be his best by Coach Hill."

## HEY NASA! BUILDING YOUNG LEADERS—A VIEW FROM THE SOCCER FIELD

*"You get the best effort from others not by lighting a fire beneath them, but by building a fire within."*
—Bob Nelson

Back during that very first year, Coach Hill started a Youth Advisory Council and Emily was part of it. Emily describes how Coach grew youth leaders: "What Coach really wanted was for the kids to help make the decisions; for the kids to help build the soccer club. He wanted them to know they had the power to create whatever type of soccer club they wanted if they chose to be leaders." He knew experiences of leadership would stay with them beyond the soccer field. He'd experienced what having leadership responsibility and recognition could do for someone and wanted to give that chance to young people on the team.

Emily has always looked to be a leader. She knows what it is to be a leader. And so much of that she's learned from Coach Hill. She's learned from what he says, and how he says it; from how he showed up every day at practice.

"I've learned so much about leadership and that's what really inspired me about Coach Hill—that he is such a leader."

In fact, during one of the Women's World Cup games in Canada, Coach inspired Emily to step out and start a movement; literally. Coach Hill suggested to Emily to start a "wave" around the stadium. A wave only requires one person to start and Emily was that person: "It was pretty exciting, because we actually got it to go all the way around the stadium. And I was the first person to start it. It was amazing. It went around seven times."

Then Coach said, "That's what you call leadership."

Emily remembers Coach always saying, "Don't worry about mistakes. What we're doing is preparing for the tournament." The focus was always about getting better for the tournament; about winning the championship. It was on taking the long view.

"One thing that showed us he is a professional coach happened at the end of the season. He told us he doesn't believe in getting trophies if you don't win the championship." Instead, Emily got a plaque. "It shows that he's very professional . . . unlike many other coaches that give you a trophy for just playing. You had to earn the trophy by winning. You might think that made it a tough environment for the kids, but it didn't. He just wanted each of us to do our personal best. And, that was very individual."

Coach did not want the kids to compare themselves to others. Rather, he wanted them to think about how they could improve to become their "personal best."

"He gave us ways to measure that improvement. That was one way I think he inspired us as individual players."

Coach Hill found something special about each of the kids on the teams. When Emily first started playing soccer, he recognized her as really smart. He told her he thought she was really intelligent and one of the smartest people on the team. One day Coach Hill asked what Emily wanted to do when she grew up. "I want to work for NASA." From that point forward, Coach Hill called her "NASA;" a fitting name for a young girl that wants to become an astrophysicist working for NASA.

"That was my name. Nobody really knew my real name when we started the club. It was always 'NASA' because he knew that I wanted to lead at NASA. Every day he called me 'NASA.'" It encouraged Emily to work hard so she could reach her goal of working for NASA.

A lot of the girls would ask Emily if NASA was her middle name. She just replied, "No, my name's Emily. Coach gave me that name because he felt like it fit me and because I said I wanted to run NASA."

Coach never gave that nickname to a single other person. It was just Emily, and that made her feel special and recognized. Although Coach Hill made Emily feel unique, there were so many kids on the club's teams and Coach knew each and every one of them. He knew what they wanted, what their dreams were for their lives. Then he did specific things to encourage them in that direction.

"Generally his message to every kid was, 'You're going to do great things with your life.' He said that consistently to every kid, whenever there was an opportunity. He said it with sincerity, with power."

Encouragement often went beyond words. "There was one kid who wanted to become a pediatrician. Coach Hill was making plans with her to meet with a doctor he knew. There were always those little connections that he was making to help kids succeed. The only reason he could do that was because he took the time to get to know the kids and understand what it was that they wanted to do in their lives."

For Emily, that experience of leading was really cool and really fun. At 12 Emily is on her way to becoming an astrophysicist. She plans on attending University of California Berkeley. She knows it's a tough school to get into, but she knows she has what it takes to succeed.

# COMMUNITY IMPACT—CHANGING A LOCAL NEIGHBORHOOD

*"What is the difference between an obstacle and an opportunity? Our attitude toward it. Every opportunity has a difficulty, and every difficulty has an opportunity."*—J. Sidlow Baxter

It hasn't just been kids and parents that have been changed in Carson City as a result of Ian's commitment and passion. Neighborhoods have changed, too.

Paris Park is located in a neighborhood of Carson City that has its fair share of challenges. Many families in that area are poor. Nearly 100% of the youth from that area qualify for free and reduced lunch at school— meaning they live well below the poverty level.

There are problems with gangs and drugs and blight in that specific neighborhood. There weren't even any bathrooms at the site for youth or parents to use, but this was the neighborhood where Coach Hill's kids would go and play soccer.

Where others saw a barrier, Coach saw an opportunity. There was a benefit to playing at that park, in that neighborhood. The soccer teams were attracting other kids and people from that neighborhood who got connected. Because kids from this neighborhood could walk to practices, their parents could get involved as well.

Even so, the neighborhood was not initially welcoming to Coach Hill and the parents. When they first started dropping their kids off for practice they heard the comments being made by some of the people walking by—people not affiliated with soccer, but that lived in the neighborhood. It made them nervous. One mom wondered if she should take her daughter and leave the park based on the comments. Yet, she stayed.

After a while the park itself started to transform. Coach and the parents paid for a portable toilet. Every month they had to pay a bill; but, there was now a place for kids to use a bathroom at the park.

Then they had a motor home start coming to provide a homework club. Now, every kid had a chance to get help with their homework during or before practice.

The neighborhood was better off because there were people at that field every night. The parents were coming there to do something positive.

Then boys started coming to that field and asking to see Coach, and all of a sudden there was a group of young high school boys who wanted to be part of youth soccer club. At first, it seemed as if the interest was all about the girls, but that wasn't the case. The boys were there, just wanting to be coached, and Coach made a place for them as well.

## WHAT IS POSSIBLE—COACH HILL MAKES A LASTING IMPACT

*"The price of success is hard work, dedication to the job at hand, and the determination that whether we win or lose, we have applied the best of ourselves to the task at hand."*—**Vince Lombardi**

When Sarah thinks about how Ian has impacted young people, she attributes much of it to how hard he works.

Ian really walked his talk. He put in more time, more energy, more money, more love, and more effort than anyone else. That doesn't by any means diminish what others were contributing, because there were a lot of other people doing the necessary work and supporting the soccer league. But Sarah could always look to Ian and see that he was doing his share many times over.

"I think that was inspiring for me as a parent. I think for the kids, also." Those kids and their parents saw somebody who was really committed to them, to their team; someone who was committed to them on a personal level: to be there, to show up, and to work hard.

For Sarah, it's difficult to separate what she was like before she met Coach Hill, Ian.

"I feel like so many of the ways I think about things are different because he's been a part of our lives . . . a really important part."

Coach Hill has inspired Sarah to make changes in her community and now she sees how to do it. "I can see how one person really can make a powerful change with something they truly believe in. I have a living example of that in Ian."

She also learned a lot from watching him coach. As coaches and parents everywhere know, it's hard for the team when they're doing their best and still not winning the games. It's hard for the players and it's hard for the parents. But Ian kept a leader's view.

"One of the things that he asked us to make a habit of doing in those situations was to make a game within the game. It was no longer about whether they won or lost the game, instead it came down to the plays (the game within the game). Who won that 50-50 ball? How someone shot a goal in a particular instance. Just really breaking the game down; because that's how you win a game. You get better and better at those individual pieces."

Those lessons and Ian's inspiration rippled beyond soccer for Sarah, into life lessons and approaching work. "Sure, you want to win a tournament. Sure, you want to win your game. But, it comes down to every move and what you can do in every move either to get better or to improve.

"That's how you end up winning in the long run."

Sarah could see that Ian was someone she wanted to emulate. So with that in mind, she observed him and tried to learn from him. She learned from the things he said, the things he did seemingly without even trying. "He taught us all that anything is possible. That these young girls; women really, could achieve anything."

While many other people say that anything is possible in a casual way, Coach Hill said it and *meant* it.

## EVER CHANGING TO MEET THE NEED

Over time, as the children, youth and community members' needs changed, so too did the scope of the work of *Let Them Be Kids*. Ian has started other organizations to meet those needs, including *The Changing Point,* offering speaking, seminars, and tools for engaging in direct communication and participating in hands-on community involvement with grassroots efforts across North America, and around the world. However, the work itself has remained the same.

The work has become bigger and has expanded to different communities and different questions were being answered; yet, the heart of the work remains the same.

The questions Ian and his team ask today around engagement, paths to a better future and effective intervention programs, all come back to one answer: through soccer. "When you 'dangle' the opportunity of soccer in front of them they change their behaviors."

"They will go to the tutor. They will go to their classes. They will behave right and they'll do what they're supposed to do. They will continue their education and go to the local community college. All for the chance to play soccer. And what we found is, they're excelling."

One of the lessons learned is that it *is* possible to help change the life trajectory of a currently disengaged, under-served youth. When they are provided positive leadership and structure, and a way to engage their passion for soccer, they experience success.

Ian reminds us there are different ways and models for doing this. Soccer is just one. But, the essential components remain the same. Caring, high expectations, focus on the future, and commitment to self and others.

## IAN'S INFLUENCES AND PASSION

*"There is no satisfaction that can compare with looking back across the years and finding you've grown in self-control, judgment, generosity, and unselfishness."*
—Ella Wheeler Wilcox

When asked about why he does what he does, what drives his passion for building individual and community leaders, Ian pauses, then attributes his drive to his faith and his background.

Ian is able to speak very openly these days about his past and the path he's traveled to this point. He acknowledges that much of his early drive to help others and improve the world came from wanting acceptance. Wanting to know he was worth something. That he mattered.

After a while, as he started experiencing success, his motivation for doing good in the world shifted a little. For Ian today, it's all about being a catalyst for change, making the world a better place.

"I'm usually in the background . . . And for the first time, over the last four years, I think I'm really doing it for the betterment of my soul now. But it took me some time to get [to this point and this awareness]."

## A DAUGHTER'S PERSPECTIVE

As a dad, Ian is also a role model to his own children. Over the years, they have each been involved in the work. One of his daughters has been part of the work in Canada, Africa and the U.S.

Ian knows she's proud of the soccer accomplishments, including the time Ian exceeded the world's longest speech in order to raise funds for the kids to go to Canada. She's proud of the playgrounds that now exist across Canada. And, she knows that their family really does follow through when they say they will try to help somebody. "We don't always follow through on everything else in life, but we follow through on that."

All that said, Ian knows his family has paid a price. He and his family have sacrificed personal and family time to contribute to the larger community. He knows it hasn't always been easy because his daughter has shared her feelings:

"I love my dad, and he's perfect in so many ways, but sometimes he's not. Sometimes saving the world gets in the way of being a good dad to me. I understand why he wants to save the world, I understand why he brings me along to save the world, but sometimes I'd rather he just be my dad, and he not be this world-changer." And the reason he knows she would say that is because she said it to him.

Knowing that, Ian has made changes to make sure he is home more; so his kids can participate and be part of the work, so they can just be kids.

## CLARITY AND REMEMBERING WHY

*"You may be only one person in this world, but to one person at one time, you are the world."*—**Anonymous**

Over the past 25 years, Ian has learned a lot about what it takes to succeed.

He knows what has helped him rebound and persevere through adversity. It starts with clarity around your passion: "It must matter enough to you that you will continue against the odds and adversity." Next, Ian suggests you become knowledgeable. "Good intentions aren't good enough. Go get equipped. Learn more about your subject and about what you plan on doing. Finally, check your motivations.

"Do you want to start this thing for yourself, your ego? Or do you truly want to do it because nobody else is filling a particular need or gap?" If after working through these questions you have clarified why you want to go in a particular direction, what value you will bring, and you find you are still passionate, then and only then, will it be time to move forward. At this point you will be better equipped, able to sustain your efforts longer, and know your true motivations.

"When the going gets tough and adversity appears—as it will from time to time, revisiting and considering the answers to these questions can become a standard coping strategy for staying the course."

Once a vulnerable youth himself, he knows firsthand what it's like to have been that "at-risk" kid navigating difficult life situations and challenges. He also knows what his life would be like today if he had not had people to help and guide him; if instead, they had decided he was too small or insignificant to care about. Remembering that is what motivates Ian today to elevate, educate and enhance the lives of others. He knows what it is like to want something that seems unattainable or larger than life. It's why he has committed himself to making a difference.

Ian often relates a poem when he speaks with individuals and groups. I remember first hearing this poem from him over 20 years ago in mid-1990s. He shares it to recognize, honor, and inspire individuals and communities in the work they do. It is still as powerful today as when I first heard Ian recite it.

*I am only one,*
*but I am one.*
*I can't do everything,*
*But I can do something;*
*that which I can do,*
*I ought to do;*
*And that which I ought to do,*
*I will do.*
*Because I cannot do everything,*
*I will not refuse to do the something that I can do.*

—*Edward Everett Hale*

# CHAPTER 4
# JULIAN

*"Tough times don't last, tough people do, remember?"*
—**Gregory Peck**

Unlike Ian, Sarah and Emily, I didn't know Julian before I interviewed him for this book. I met him through a member of the online writing community. What inspires me about Julian and his story is the audacity of his goals; how when faced with adversity and uncertainty, he pushed forward then, as he continues to do so today.

I am inspired by the lessons Julian has learned along the way about the kindness of strangers, working towards a dream, and setting big goals. After years of not quite fitting in at school or with his family, he packed up his music, stuck out his thumb, and escaped with a friend to travel across the United States. Today, on top of working long, physically demanding days in construction, Julian challenges the Guinness World Record, works to build a strong family of musicians, and increases the economic viability of the local music scene in Chico, California.

# JULIAN'S BACKGROUND

*"You cannot do a kindness too soon, for you never know how soon it will be too late."*
—Ralph Waldo Emerson

Julian grew up about an hour's drive from downtown Detroit. He lived in the town of Port Huron, Michigan, where the blocks seemed to him nearly a mile long. His entire family still lives there, including his sisters and brother, mother and stepfather—the man who raised him and who he calls dad. Julian lived in a trailer park for the first half of his childhood. He describes his family as one that was full of love and good people; people who care for one another to such a degree that they're each other's best friends.

They were poor enough that it was noticed by others, including the kids and teachers at school. Julian imagines that some people even called his family white trash. They weren't though. They were poor, certainly. That was circumstantial and not a statement about their character. When Julian was about 10, his family moved out of the trailer park and onto a beautiful piece of property where they started building a home—a home that his father still lives in to this day.

Julian was a good student. He immersed himself in art and got straight A's on his report cards. He was considered a "twerp" and a nerd, though; a combination that translated into getting pushed around a lot. No question about it.

There were people who saw Julian as a kid with great potential, even while he lacked certain boundaries. A kid that they perceived to be a good investment of their time and energy.

He realized this because around the holidays and his birthday, random presents would show up at his grandmother's front door with his name on them. Presents like winter coats and board games, and other things that a kid like him might need or want.

Julian learned early on that he could count on the kindness of strangers. This knowledge doesn't often come to one at such a young age. Fortunately for Julian, it did. The knowledge that people whom he didn't know cared about him made a lasting impression on him.

Even with a good family, Julian's childhood and teen years were tough. His horror stories from 'back in the day,' include times where he'd been beaten up, and even hospitalized. His nose was replaced due to being hit so much it had "pretty much been knocked off" his face.

Julian did not really fit in. From time to time he would go "rogue." At the age of 15 Julian set out on his own. "I love my family very much. But we were very different types of people." So he moved out, and he started working for a living. Leaving home at an early age, paying rent and taking care of himself as an adult, brought with it tumultuous teen years. In fact it was so difficult at times that he even became suicidal. He clung to his music.

"Music has always been a part of my life. I have never taken a break from it." He was connected to music before he was born.

When his mother was pregnant with him, she taught herself to play guitar. She was writing songs about him when she was just 17. In the womb, he was serenaded by her songs and acoustic music. Song writing and music have been Julian's companions most of his life.

Like his mother, it wasn't until Julian was a teenager that he really picked up music composition and playing. He was in a marching band and he taught himself to play guitar. He turned his poetry into music and that became a kind of meditation and medicine for him. Music helped with some of the stress and struggles that any teen in his situation would go through. Like many teenagers, music and writing provided outlets for processing his experiences. But Julian's music evolved from processing and purging his past experiences, to becoming a source of joy and creation for the sake of the music itself.

Julian had his guitar with him when he left town.

## LEAVING TOWN

*"But if these years have taught me anything it is this: you can never run away. Not ever. The only way out is in."*
**—Junot Díaz**

When Julian turned 17 he hit the road. He'd heard about hitchhiking and it sounded like a good idea. He wanted an escape from his hometown. He stuck out his thumb and started hitchhiking around the Midwest. After a while, he returned home on a Greyhound bus. That one experience ignited his desire to travel more. The next summer he decided to hitchhike across the country. He was 18 when he and a friend hitchhiked from Michigan out to Portland, Oregon and down into Northern California.

On one of the last legs of their trip, they met a man in his 30s who was traveling to California to work for carnivals. Julian and his friend went too and joined the carnival circuit. All that summer they traveled with the carnival companies throughout northern California and through the Central Valley. These were the poor end of carnivals as they later learned; the kind of carnival where everybody saved up all week to rent a motel room just so they could take a shower.

These folks were different than Julian. While it wasn't uncommon for several of the workers to have warrants out for their arrest, Julian and his friend were fresh-faced kids from the Midwest. They just wanted to take tickets at rides, hold darts for the games, and sell the jewelry that they made. At the end of that summer, Julian and his friend returned home to Michigan and back into their separate lives.

## INTO THE NAVY

Then Julian joined the Navy where he turned another corner on the path to adulthood and encountered the after effects of his youth. He learned how the darkness and challenges he had faced growing up as a teenager came back to haunt him, especially when put in rigid, psychologically demanding circumstances; the routine situations encountered in boot camp.

The recruits were sleeping 3 to 4 hours a night, and sleep deprivation coupled with the physical demands of boot camp was taking its toll. The experience pushed Julian. He found himself struggling emotionally. At a certain point, that became obvious to the people around him as well.

After two months at boot camp, he found himself sitting across from an officer at Great Lakes Navy Boot Camp, and he was presented with a choice. Did he want to go home or continue in boot camp? The officer said he could stay, but indicated he was a great case to leave the service.

Sitting there on the western shore of Lake Michigan, just 30 miles north of O'Hare Airport, he chose an honorable discharge and left the Navy.

## FROM CARNIVALS TO CLOTHING OPTIONAL

You never know where you will end up or when one decision will present a new opportunity. That's what happened for Julian. He returned to work the carnival circuit in California with the same company. It was two years later and this time a different friend accompanied him. At the end of the summer, Julian gave his car to his friend to drive back to Michigan while Julian stayed behind.

He moved into a clothing-optional Buddhist/Hindu Meditation Retreat Center in Northern California. The center catered to a different group of people than he'd been working with on the carnival circuit. Within the span of a week, Julian went from trying to convince people to take a chance at winning a prize by throwing a basketball into a hoop, to washing dishes, wearing a sarong and flip flops while surrounded by naked people.

That retreat center was the first place Julian ever lived in California. It was the first place he settled and connected. While it was quite a change for a kid from rural Michigan, Julian has never left California.

For most of the past decade, Julian has earned his living doing fence construction. He creates and builds from wood, iron, and chain-links. He does commercial and residential projects, big jobs, small jobs. And when he's done with his work day, Julian comes home and dives into his passion: music.

## MUSIC: THE UNWAVERING CONNECTION

*"If you look into someone's life—your own life, you will likely find a theme, a thread, something that has been a part of you ever since you were young. It could be a hobby. An interest area, like nature, hiking, cars, building, art, and reading . . . it could be anything. But, it will be the one thing that you come back to when you need to feel grounded, or connected, or safe. Music has been with me the entire time."*
**—Julian Ruck**

Julian reached beyond writing and performing his songs to also doing stand-up comedy, which is not really a big stretch for Julian. He saw how comics used the stage and their performances to make fun of and help themselves and others battle their shadow sides. He recognized from observing the paths traveled by Hollywood celebrities that he could either follow in their footsteps and use drugs or take pills to cope with his own past; or, he could use the stage as his medicine.

The stage and performance won out.

"I love entertaining people. I love making people dance and making people happy."

Of himself and this time of his life he says, "I'm really the happiest I've ever been and it's been an organic process. One that makes me confident that the trend will continue."

## GOING FOR GUINNESS — THE IDEA

*"There is no such thing as can't."*—Christopher Reeve

With such a strong connection to music, it might not seem like such a leap to think about Julian's big challenge to himself: get Chico and its large community of musicians recognized for the talent they are.

Julian had already been promoting his friends' music, in addition to his own, throughout the community. He created a singer songwriter super group that made three albums together. It was a collaborative project where everybody contributed equally. They played on each other's songs and sang back up for one another. They became a song writer super-group.

Then Julian partnered with a friend of his to create the I Play in Chico local music documentary.

*I Play in Chico* (IPiC) is a not-for-profit documentary[11] about Chico's local music scene. Filmed over the course of two months, it features over a hundred of some of the area's most talented artists, along with interviews.

Initially, the friend's plan had been to produce a 5 minute commercial of the local music scene. But after only a few short weeks of production it became clear that the video had more potential than a 5 minute commercial. So, six months later, a 50 minute documentary about the Chico music scene was released on You Tube called *I Play in Chico*.

It was only the first step. At the same time he was working on the video, Julian had a bigger vision for what could be possible for Chico and its music scene.

He started by asking himself what he could do to bring more music lovers to Chico. He knew the community was inspired by the beautiful scenery and a town everyone loves to live in. He wondered what might be done to encourage people to visit and stay in Chico longer. He wanted to drive enough interest in the local community to grow and support the music scene.

Then he asked himself a question that merged the two ideas.

What if, in addition to the documentary, they staged the longest concert in the world? Featuring all of the local musicians, the different genres of music and showcasing the richness that already exists in Chico? How long would that concert have to be?

He set about learning what it would take to put on such a concert. First, he learned what the longest concert in the world had been to date. According to Guinness Book of World Records it was 15 days and 12 hours. He knew he could pull that off without a hitch. Over the years he'd watched the local warm-up bands that consistently wanted to play just "one more song" in their set before stepping aside for an out of town headliner act. Julian was confident he wouldn't have any trouble exceeding the world record by an hour. It would only require 373 hours of music—a little more than 15 and half days. After years of focusing on the local music scene, he knew there were hundreds of bands in town. He had all the local talent he needed.

But his idea wasn't merely to exceed the world record by a couple of hours. That had already been done a couple of times before. Rather, it was to exceed it in such a way that it would shine a spotlight on Chico and the local music scene, he dreamed of exceeding it permanently.

During the filming of *I Play in Chico*, Julian had been telling people about the Guinness record attempt idea. He shared with people that the Guinness attempt had been his dream since the previous summer. He revealed how he recognized first hand that a lot of local bands were getting passed over for the national bands that come through town. He shared how the local bars were invested heavily in national acts; and, how those interests and investments sent thousands of dollars out of the area, while it left talented local musicians sitting on the sidelines.

The more he shared his ideas, the more committed he became to promoting local music and directing work and resources to local musicians and bands. He knew it would ultimately benefit the Chico community, its music and arts scenes, and small businesses.

He sent messages to Guinness to let them know he intended to *double* the world record. He obtained the rules; there were many. He studied them throughout the filming of *I Play in Chico*. He found a venue away from the downtown area with owners who were ambitious in their own right, already taking down walls and building a stage and a new dance floor. Although the location was known as a country bar, Julian saw from having grown up in rural Michigan that those venues were perfect. They were often a kind of "catch all" for music. They are a place where you can throw peanuts on the floor; where almost any kind of music can be viable given the circumstance. And, almost anybody can be comfortable. These types of places often had a Garth Brooks, "friends in low places" kind of vibe.

Following a suggestion from a friend, Julian approached the owners with the idea almost immediately after he contacted Guinness for the rules. The owners were instantly on board.

With a venue secured, Julian turned his entire focus to learning the rules. He poured over them in order to plan every detail. He didn't want to jeopardize the attempt for lack of understanding a requirement.

The rules were stringent and specific. What would it take to qualify as the longest concert?

No more than 30 seconds between songs. No more than 5 minutes between acts. If a set change is scheduled, it has to happen fast. After reviewing these requirements, it became clear to Julian why most of the previous attempts to set the world record were primarily accomplished by songwriters in a coffee house with perhaps 50 musicians on a rotation. No large bands participated and the music tended to be acoustic.

That would not work for Chico.

"We had to design our concert to include full on bands: nine piece, 10 piece, and even a 12 piece band. At one point we even had a choir of 25."

Julian did not want to tell bands and musicians that they couldn't play simply because it would be too complicated. He had to figure out a way to have the bands and musicians play while adhering to the

Guinness timing requirements. He started with "yes" then went about planning to make it happen.

## GOING FOR GUINNESS—A PARTNERSHIP EMERGES

*"Alone we can do so little; together we can do so much."*—**Helen Keller**

Amidst the frenzy, the hard work and commitment that it took to envision, plan and launch the Guinness world record attempt emerged a partnership that would become essential to the pursuit.

Two years prior when Julian was co-hosting a segment on local radio, he interviewed a young woman named Emily about a book she was writing. This was the same time Julian was trying to get volunteer teams together for the Guinness world record attempt. He had over one hundred volunteers signed up. Each volunteer committed to attending two meetings per week, starting 60 days before the event. Dozens of people were showing up. Inspired by the project, Emily came to a Tuesday volunteer meeting.

That particular evening, she was the only volunteer.

Although they barely knew each other, they started working closely together on the project. Emily was very talented, bringing her skills in marketing, social media, writing, graphic and website design, and solid business expertise. On top of that, she brought her enthusiasm. Together they poured over plans, sponsorship, and ad campaigns in order to launch the event.

While, Julian had put the wheels in motion on the Guinness world record attempt, it was Emily's arrival on the scene that allowed him to have a much needed co-director.

"She was working 30 hours a week or more with me. There's no doubt that the project was much more successful because of her involvement."

## GOING FOR GUINNESS — THE MUSIC, THE PEOPLE, THE COMPLAINTS

The floodgates had been opened. Everybody who wanted to play started making their interest known to Julian. That's also when some people decided they wanted to control who should be allowed to play, and when and how that should happen. There were those who wanted to limit some types of music to hours when fewer people would be inclined to participate. Or, to avoid certain days of the week that have traditionally been known for a particular type of music. Julian wasn't having any of it. It didn't fit his vision of an inclusive music scene.

Julian's response to the various requests was an emphatic "No." It would be difficult enough to get people coordinated and engaged without adding an unnecessary degree of complication to the already complex scheduling. The event needed to be "come one, come all." Musicians were not to be excluded. Julian understood he upset some people with the decisions that he made, people who had very specific and special needs that, should he accommodate them would be unfair to others to accommodate. He found himself in a position where he had to put the community first, over any particular person's wishes. That posed a real challenge, but it also showed him who he could count on—the people who would really step up and come to the floor to achieve results.

The owners of the venue agreed to the come-one-come-all approach and increased their staffing in order to accommodate the bigger, more inclusive vision.

Julian also recognized it wasn't just the venue and the musicians he needed to engage in a successful record attempt. There were city and county ordinances and public perception to address. He started going to City Council meetings several months before the event to share with the council members and the community about the attempt, where it would be held, and the benefits to the community. He assured them that the venue would stop serving alcohol at 2 a.m. They would keep the doors open for the event and host a breakfast buffet. The members of the Council and the public were invited to come by whenever they wanted.

Julian was intentional in his communications.

The goal of the World Record attempt was threefold: first, it was to *double* the current world record; second, Julian wanted to shed light on and promote Chico's local music scene; and third, Julian wanted to bring forth positive news about Chico—to be recognized both nationally and internationally for something good. Certain perceptions about the Chico community still lingered. Formed over the years as a result of negative events making national news, these events did not portray the full picture of the community.

Even though many years had passed since the hazing death at a fraternity, a shooting death and a train fatality, reputations die hard. What Julian wanted the council members and the public to understand was how this event—the attempt to break a Guinness World Record—could highlight what Chico truly is.

"It is a music town and a food town, and it's our town. It is a budding town [within] a mature town, and a progressive town. Chico is big enough to have musical diversity. But it is not so big that the different genres are segregated, as they often are in larger cities. It's really that sweet spot in the population size. There is a lot of creative energy in this area of Northern California."

There were artists who Julian had tried to recruit who declined. Some told him they didn't think it was a good idea for the local music scene to do something like the Guinness attempt. Others just declined. But within two weeks of the launch, those musicians would be asking when they could play.

## LET THE RECORD ATTEMPT BEGIN

It was finally time to begin the Guinness record attempt after months of planning. There were still loose ends but the time to launch the event was upon them. Even with all the local talent available and months of planning and preparation, the first 24 hours of the attempt had not been booked by the time the music started. They had announced the start date and time so at 8:30 p.m. on April 1, 2015 it was 'all systems go.' They had enough music booked to carry them through to 2:00 a.m. But, no one booked beyond that time. Some musicians were still waiting to see if the attempt would succeed before jumping on board. Some just said they would play but hadn't confirmed. Julian, Emily and the volunteers had to trust that people would show up and play. Julian would be the backup plan.

From the start, Julian had been prepared to jump on stage and play for six hours every night—even in the middle of the night, if that's what it would take. But "heroic efforts" on the music front would not be necessary. Within a few days word spread about the attempt. They hadn't done much promotion because they believed the town was small enough that if the music community connected with one another, word-of-mouth would do the trick to carry the message, and local musicians would come to play.

That's what happened. Local musicians and those from outside the Chico area wanted to join the attempt. Delhi 2 Dublin, a world music group formed in 2006 in Vancouver, Canada performed in the middle of the night. Coolio, the American Grammy Award-winning musician, rapper, actor, and record producer, performed at 3:30 in the morning. Julian found himself on stage rapping with him. Unplanned, unexpected, and amazing. Everybody played for free. The only exceptions were the bands that had already been booked months before for two-hour sets scheduled for Friday and Saturday nights. Although they were paid, they also had to follow the Guinness rules. They had to adjust their sets to accommodate; and, they were all willing to do that.

Where help would be needed was maintaining the required audience levels.

In addition to continuous music, the Guinness rules require that a minimum of 10 people be in the crowd at all times. Never fewer.

This ended up being one of the most challenging parts of the entire contest. Unlike having a musician ready to step in and play at a moment's notice, they didn't have a contingency plan for keeping the minimum number of audience members in attendance at all times.

"Honestly, we could probably have gotten musicians to play for years . . . but maintaining 10 people in the audience was really challenging, especially at 4:00 or 5:00 a.m., on a Tuesday."

After the first few days, people told him he could stop the Guinness attempt, that he'd made his mark on the local music scene. Stopping was never a consideration for Julian. He knew there were hundreds of acts to come. Easily half of the artists were people he'd never seen or heard of in his life. Those musicians needed a stage and Julian intended to give them one.

The music affected people even after they left the venue. People told Julian that even when they weren't there to hear and experience the music live, they felt there was "an umbilical cord of their song speaking." They felt deeply connected. The Guinness attempt continued on.

Then the road got a little bumpy.

The work was so intense, the communications so frequent, that once the event started, Julian lost his voice within the first two weeks.

Julian couldn't perform. He had to make a video asking people to do their own research and find answers to questions about the event. It was all so that he wouldn't have to use his voice.

# RESETTING THE CLOCK/LOSS OF POWER

*"Some things are beyond our control. A power outage is one of them."*—**Julian Ruck**

Four and a half days into the attempt, the power went out throughout the region. More than 80,000 people lost power, including the venue. Immediately people started arriving to see if the record attempt would continue. People came with their cell phones to capture video of the ongoing event to use as documentation in support of the record attempt.

When they lost power Julian had to make a decision. He would have turned to Emily, but she had gone home to get some much needed sleep. Should he chance that Guinness would accept the alternative documentation, due the changed circumstances? Or, should he risk the community's anger and frustration and start over?

He decided to reset the clock. He couldn't risk that continuing without doing so would put the rest of the attempt in jeopardy.

A blue grass band was playing when the power went out; and, they continued playing their set acoustically. From beginning to end, the concert never stopped. They just didn't officially count the first four and a half days.

It turned out that the power outage was a blessing, in disguise.

The nationally syndicated Bob and Tom radio show took note. The show features news, sports, lifestyle content, and interviews with actors, authors and newsmakers. It features live performances from singers, songwriters, and musicians coming from all genres of music. In short, its audience cares about music. The Guinness attempt was of particular interest.

Bob and Tom made comments about the Guinness world record attempt in Chico, California that was interrupted by the power outage. "We were 4 or 5 days in at that point and, at least for a moment [there was] some national news of our effort." It bolstered awareness and energy.


## LOSS OF POWER—AGAIN

As they neared the end of the record attempt, there was another power outage.

One of the previously booked weekend bands hired by the venue decided they didn't want to be a part of the record attempt. They wanted to play the way they always did without conforming to Guinness rules. In order to keep the Guinness attempt going, Julian had to quickly adapt. Immediately they moved the performances to the back patio of the venue. This is where they would play for the next 12 hours, until they could return to the inside stage. Again, it worked to their advantage.

"While we were performing in the back patio, the power went out again. This time it was because the big band on the indoor stage was pulling so much power that all the equipment went down."

Luck was on the side of Julian and the local musicians. Since they were playing a more intimate setting and primarily acoustic, it only required a single generator to keep the music playing. Had they been playing the inside stage when the power went out, it's likely the attempt would have ended, just shy of the few days needed to double the record.

Finally, after 34 days and 20 hours the concert part of the contest came to a close.


## THE EVIDENCE ACROSS AMERICA TOUR

*"It always seems impossible until it's done."*
**—Nelson Mandela**

As much work that had gone in prior to the event, documenting after the event was just as intense, if not more so. Julian had put months of energy into the preparation, information gathering, and sponsor solicitation prior to volunteer involvement. After the event, volunteers shouldered the heavy workload so Julian could go back to work and try to rebuild his savings after not working for six weeks. Gathering the evidence and documentation they would need to prove to Guinness they had met the standards and exceeded the existing world record translated into 50 hour weeks for Emily, and hundreds of volunteer hours. One particular volunteer spent 100 hours on categorizing. That's how they verified there were **900 musicians** on stage and **11,000 songs** performed.

When it was time to send the materials to New York (to the Guinness offices) they had an idea: drive to New York and hand the evidence over in person. They had calculated the costs to ship the materials and it would be the same as the gas to travel across the country. They decided to drive.

They called it "The Evidence across America Tour." Over the course of three weeks they stopped at open mics and jam nights in 20 cities along the way. In each of these cities Julian got his guitar and either played original music or joined the jam that was in progress; all to spread the word about what they had just accomplished in Chico, California.

"It was like an advertising victory lap around the country. We would tell people that the prior record was 15 days and 12 hours. Then we tell them we just completed **34 days and 20 hours**. Without fail they would be amazed." The whole point of the trip was to rebrand Chico as a music town. The tour really helped set the stage.

Hand delivering the documentation evidence to Guinness has its own crazy story.

Julian and Emily barely made it at the last minute on a Friday. As Julian was carrying 60 pounds of evidence along with his luggage through Times Square, navigating 12 long city blocks, sweating, Emily was running ahead; all to get to Guinness before the close of business. She made it ahead of Julian and convinced a guy to stay late on a Friday. Julian arrived with the boxes just in time to be chastised about the last minute delivery on a Friday, at the end of a long week. To which they responded, "It's the first possible minute this [documentation] could have been delivered here." It was a gamble taking the materials directly to the New York office.

The binders were full of witness paperwork and terabytes of audio video. There was additional backup documentation and materials to support the attempt. It wasn't until they had actually handed the documentation over that they were 100 percent sure they would be received at the New York location. It was not Guinness' policy. Yet, it was worth the risk.

Emily and Julian wanted to meet someone—an actual person—from Guinness. They wanted that personal interaction. To share the story of the *Evidence across America Tour*. They wanted Guinness to have a point of reference, some faces to connect with the world record attempt to double the longest music event;

some actual participants and residents of Chico that believed and invested in the dream.

They departed leaving behind an insane amount of evidence and documentation. They believed they dropped off more evidence for an attempt than had ever been submitted before. Simply because most Guinness continuous concert records are broken over a single day or perhaps even two, but not as long as 34 or 35 days.

## NO GUARANTEES, THE WAITING BEGINS

Immediately after delivering the documentation, the waiting started. According to Guinness procedures, it would be at least three long, restless months before they heard any news.

"There's no question we were playing for 34 days and 20 hours nonstop." However, it would likely not be enough to meet the requirements.

The truth is there were performance errors almost every day. When Julian had to make a judgment call he always chose creating community over anything else. It may have impacted their chances of success with Guinness.

All music is supposed to be rehearsed. But there were times when musicians were on stage and an artist started jamming, it then became freestyle. It was still music. It was still nonstop playing. But since the rules don't officially allow for that, the outcome was uncertain when they turned in the documentation. When Julian saw a young man in his 30s playing jazz guitar and an old man in his 80s playing jazz piano, beginning to jam together, Julian wasn't going to say no. That's the power of connection. They had hoped that Guinness perceived the spirit of the event as being intact, but sadly, that didn't happen.

After hearing nothing for months, Julian started calling Guinness without results. It was after he called a Guinness Vice President that he received two messages: first, the evidence was received; but second, the attempt was denied due to insufficient evidence. Julian was not deterred. He is the type of person that prefers to see barriers or disappointments as learning experiences. He sees the deeper connections, and some of the intangible things that came out of the Guinness attempt as successes in and of themselves.

## CHANGED BY EXPERIENCES AND OUTCOMES

*"You just can't beat the person who won't give up."*
**—Babe Ruth**

When the first attempt was all said and done, Julian stepped back and took stock of what, up to now he considers the greatest accomplishment of his life. From the beginning, Julian just felt the attempt would be successful. He didn't have actual numbers to back it up at the beginning, and in some respects it was just an educated guess of what was possible. However, he was confident that the community would get behind the Guinness record attempt and support it.

He also expected that the host venue would potentially make an extra $10–$15,000 a month from the event. His hope was that at the end of it, the owners would know hosting it was worth their time; and it turned out that it was worth it, since they made more than four times what Julian had hoped.

More important than financial gains, or even breaking the Guinness record, the real achievements were the ways in which the event touched people's lives. Julian found himself humbled by various people's experiences at the event.

"There were grey haired dudes with their country guitar who hadn't played on a stage in 20 years. They came down from the hill to be a part of this thing." There were people, particularly older people who expressed to Julian that their life had been opened, as once again they saw themselves as musicians. Some had already scheduled themselves for an upcoming jam session.

There was one musician who played almost every day for the event. She played on stage with her Dad, who she hadn't spoken with in four years. Every single day, something amazing would happen.

Now a year later, Julian still has people telling him how much the event meant to them and how excited they have become about Chico's local music scene.

"We recently found out about a couple who are now together because of the event. They met at the event. They are now engaged, and they have a baby on the way. All because of the event."

As would be expected of someone trying to build, promote and grow the music scene, Julian's real concern was how the community would take the news if Guinness rejected the attempt. His hope was that they wouldn't consider themselves deceived or misled. And they didn't. Instead, they recognized what they had accomplished and how powerful the event had been, whether or not it was recognized by Guinness.

After hearing that the evidence had been rejected, Julian asked the community whether they wanted him to initiate the appeal process. However, after learning more about the process and hearing horror stories of those who had appealed, they decided not to. There was no appetite for focusing on the past.

"Personally, I feel like I owe the community a 'win'. I've never been the kind of person to stay down. In fact, when I was in grade school and getting beat up and knocked down, people would say to me 'just stay down.'" He didn't stay down then and he didn't stay down after hearing Guinness' decision.

Rather, they took what they learned, raised their game and dove right back in. Things are already different this year.

## CHICO STRIKES BACK

*"Twenty years from now you will be more disappointed by the things that you didn't do than by the ones you did do. So throw off the bowlines. Sail away from the safe harbour. Catch the trade winds in your sails. Explore. Dream. Discover."*—**Mark Twain**

On April 1, 2016—exactly one year to the day after the first attempt, a second World Record attempt in Chico began, dubbed *Chico Strikes Back*. Julian laughs and quotes an old Arab proverb that underscores his new approach, "Trust in God but tie up your Camel."[12] Julian recognizes that it's one thing to have faith and trust in destiny, but as a wiser man today, he also knows it's up to him to do whatever he can to ensure a successful outcome.

"We have made huge modifications to our processes and documentation." For starters, Julian is operating under his new business license as the "World's Longest Concert." They are using live streaming to document the musicians and the audience; they are hosting it on YouTube. Everything is computerized. Gone is reliance on paper-based documentation and still photographs. And, rather than doubling the length of the longest concert, they are going to beat it by only half a day—a mere 12 hours.

"For us, that will be a piece of cake. We already know how to go 34 days—so, 12 extra hours won't be hard at all."

Only a day and half into this year's attempt, they are seeing the difference. This year's venue is downtown. They had to turn people away after the first two hours as they were already at capacity. They have music booked for the next two weeks. And, in addition to meeting all of the Guinness standards, they've added some of their own.

## BEYOND CHICO AND GUINNESS LIES THE NEXT DREAM

The whole point of the Guinness attempt was to bring attention to the local music scene in Chico. The region was losing artists to other places because there wasn't enough competition and it [Guinness] generated that interest. "We brought the event to town. The event happened. The results exceeded expectations that first year. Instead of the extra $15,000, [the venue] made closer to *$45,000*. The venue's Facebook page grew from "100 people were here" to "13,000 people were here." There were **900 musicians** involved, representing more than **300 separate acts**."

Now all over town, restaurants and coffee houses, and places that had said they would never offer live music, are now doing just that. The event started a fire.

"If even five percent more locals go out to live shows more often because of the Guinness attempt, then the event was a win."

That's exactly what has been happening. "More and more restaurants are getting their music license. There are many more places to play than there used to be."

Julian is already looking ahead to 2017 and his vision for that year's contest.

In June 2016, he begins a nine and a half month trip to visit 140 cities across America. Traveling by bus and train, carrying his ukulele and guitar, he will be promoting the National Endurance Concert (based on the Chico standard). In his travels he will talk with musicians, music promoters and venues to identify cities and communities to participate. As with all his record attempts, the 2017 event will start April 1, 2017.

Julian has a challenge for us all:

1. If you are inspired by the dream of *I Play in Chico* (IPiC) and what music can do for a community, then take what lessons the Chico community has learned and apply them to your town or city. If you want to be part of the 2017

concert challenge, message him on his
Facebook page at Julian Ruck.[13]

2. When people you know bring up Chico—talk
about our music.

3. If you are inspired to action, then go inspire
others.

## PERSONAL HEROES AND INSPIRATION

Who are Julian's heroes? Who influenced him the
most growing up? Who influences him today?

Those are not simple answers for Julian. There are
almost too many of them to name one single person.
He points to Martin Luther King, Jr. as an example of
one personal hero when he was growing up.

Julian is quick to point out that in today's society he
believes we each have to be our own hero. So, he looks
closer to home, to his community and to other
communities.

When Julian looks to his own community for
inspiration, he looks to Stacey Wear and Gerard
Ungerman (both featured in this book) and the work
they are doing through *Respectful Revolution*. He is
inspired by their passion for traveling the country and
documenting stories of everyday people who are doing
amazing things.

When it comes to music today, Julian draws his inspiration from a number of people who use their music to bring people together.

He notes the lineage of musicianship in the culture that's doing just that. Jackson Browne is one of the people Julian admires. In addition to his music, Jackson advocates on behalf of the environment, human rights, and arts education. He's a co-founder of multiple nonprofit organizations, including the *Success Through the Arts Foundation*, which provides education opportunities for students in South Los Angeles.[14]

Then there's Jake Shimabukuro[15] who is a world-class ukulele player. Julian learned that Jake did an entire tour where half of his proceeds went to help get water to villages. Jake continues in this work. In 2009, Jake performed with Bette Midler in the presence of Her Majesty the Queen as part of a special fundraising concert in Blackpool, England.[16] He is playing with the Hawaii Symphony Orchestra Concertmaster and violinist Ignace "Iggy" Jang to benefit Hawaii Performing Arts Festival.

And then, there are the people who put spiritual energy behind their music: Bob Marley and John Lennon.

"I am inspired by lyrics and songs that take a look at the bigger picture."

## VALUES AND FOCUS

Over the years Julian has been able to navigate change and challenge. No longer a Christian, he relies on a few core values he learned as a child that have stayed with him. For instance:

"Do unto others as you would have them do unto you," and "He who sins throws the first stone." Along with the basic principles of consciousness like putting yourself in someone else's shoes, not being selfish, and striving to be humble at the same time that you strive to fulfill your unique purpose in this world.

"[Often times] I think that when people are struggling to find their purpose, they're more focused on recognition rather than purpose . . . because your purpose is literally your neighborhood, friends."

Julian shared a major lesson he has learned by telling a story of another man. "This man tried to save the world in his 20's. He tried to save his city in his 30's. Then he tried to save his state and region in his 40's, and on and on until finally he realized he had it backwards. The man should have started with saving himself, then his friends, family, and his community, and after that his state. Then, just maybe then, he would have had a chance at changing the world."

These are some of the fundamental principles Julian is grounded in.

# ADVICE TO HIS 10-YEAR-OLD SELF

*"The big picture doesn't just come from distance; it also comes from time."*—**Simon Sinek**

It's one thing to be an adult and know that you can navigate challenges and disappointments. It's another to be a young boy going through so much with no knowledge of the future; a boy with no idea that in just a couple of decades he will be attempting to break a world record.

What advice would Julian offer his 10-year old self?

"Well, because of my past I do have a real soft spot for at risk teens or people who struggle in their youth. I've thought about this question quite a bit and I think the most important thing to impress on young people is that it gets better."

"I think that very often young people who are feeling frustrated, suicidal, depressed—all those things, are surrounded by adults that aren't happy either. [So], they do not see that it gets better."

He would also be honest with his 10-year-old self. From his current vantage point, Julian knows it's much better to be honest. He doesn't think it's helpful when adults or parents tell kids that the glory days were when they were young."

Instead, he would tell young Julian this:

"You get to pay bills, you get to have your own place, you get to go eat wherever you want, you get to work, you get to make money, you get to rely on yourself, and you get to do anything you want."

He might even share what it was like for him as a teenager when he was suicidal, and how scenes from *Pump up the Volume*[17] changed his viewpoint and set him on a new path. In one particular scene, Mark confronts the issue of suicide by telling his listeners to "do something about their problems, rather than submitting to them and surrendering through committing suicide. Just do something nuts. No one in your life wants you to kill yourself. Just walk away. Just move to another country, get on a boat. Just do anything else other than commit suicide."

"[It was] that kind of mentality that got me sticking out my thumb." And that saved Julian's life.

"Based on my experience, I would tell somebody that's in a tough spot, 'It is only going to get brighter. It's only going to get better . . . and being an adult is fantastic.'"

# BEYOND JUST GETTING BY

*"The focus should be on acknowledging that you are lucky to be alive. Period. Then beyond that you're lucky because you can do whatever you want with your life. It's yours."*—**Julian Ruck**

Julian acknowledges how hard it was for him as a teenager and young adult. Ultimately, Julian sees how these experiences have led to his desire to create community and to give back to others.

"People say, "I've always relied on the kindness of strangers", and that's been really, really true in my life."

Some of those strangers were people he met in books. When times were at their darkest, Julian read. There were times where books were his "only friends." Philosophy, religion and other such topics appealed to him. His reading helped form what he considers pretty solid personal beliefs about consciousness and existence.

"I believe we are each powerful in ways that we can't even comprehend. People too often get wrapped up in asking "What's my purpose? What am I supposed to do with my life? What am I supposed to do?"

"'Shoulds and regrets', guilt and other emotions like that get in the way. The focus should be on acknowledging that you are lucky to be alive. Period.

Then beyond that you're lucky because you can do whatever you want with your life. It's yours."

Now, when Julian looks back over the years he can see how his life has improved: day by day; week by week; month by month. His life has consistently gotten better since he was a kid.

His life experiences—the painful and the pleasant—have influenced who he is today. Having been on the receiving end of so much help over the years has motivated Julian to consistently look for ways to give help to others. His passion for helping the local music scene and the musicians in Chico is just one example, another is his tour across America to promote the work and artistry of local musicians across the U.S.

Julian is no different than anybody else. Staying motivated can be harder some days than others. What has really helped him is to ignore criticism, and not to take things personally. He focuses on what he sets out to do, continuing to put one foot in front of the other.

"Tuning out criticism. That's a key for staying motivated, organized and moving forward."

"I tend to stay pretty motivated. I have good people around me. Good people I'm working with—and that motivates me."

"I feel like that really right now I'm at the happiest, best, most successful, accomplished, motivated, and confident than I've ever been."

# CHAPTER 5
# MICHELLE

*"The power of one man or one woman doing the right thing for the right reason, and at the right time, is the greatest influence in our society."*—Jack Kemp

I first met Michelle Jezycki nearly 25 years ago. I was running a small nonprofit agency and Michelle was a truant officer with the Washoe County school district, in Reno Nevada. We encountered each as part of a county-wide multidisciplinary team to develop a plan for protecting missing and exploited children. Even today, I remember Michelle's energy, passion and her commitment to helping young people, and her determination to improve the systems that are supposed to protect and serve children as inspiring. She was a natural at bringing people together, having fun while working hard, and getting everyone going in the same direction toward a goal. When we traveled to other communities to help them create similar plans to protect missing and exploited children, her energy, expertise and knowledge encouraged others to work together. People were motivated to cross the artificial barriers of professional turf in favor of doing what was right on behalf of youth.

Throughout her life, Michelle has demonstrated a commitment to encouraging and building people up.

She did this as a kid in school and as a young woman in college. She focused on helping others when she was just beginning her professional career and working as a school truant officer. Her commitment to helping others followed her when she moved to Washington, DC and started working with the National Center for Missing and Exploited Children, and again when she was hired as the Director of Human Resources for the United States Senate. Today, Michelle owns a travel agency serving triathletes around the world, teaches for the National Institute of Health, and is a private consultant and coach working both nationally and internationally.

Leadership—Nature or Nurture? It is a question frequently asked: Are leaders made or born? When it comes to Michelle, it may be a bit of both. As far back as people remember, Michelle has been a leader. At the same time, she has definitely been shaped by her environment.

Family stories of Michelle as a kid point to her being an early leader.

*"If your actions inspire others to dream more, learn more, do more and become more, you are a leader."*
**—John Quincy Adams**

When a storm brought in so much snow that they closed the schools, Michelle took the lead. She started by asking her siblings and the half dozen cousins that were staying with them at the time, "Okay, how are we going to entertain ourselves?"

They decided to make a video.

Michelle organized everyone and took charge of making the video, including commercials. Actors included her twin who was washing her hair and promoting shampoo. When they cut to the news segment, Michelle had her twin typing away, making sound effects for a "just breaking now" news feed with that tap, tap, tap, typing sound. Then the band of cousins, each with a role, created their version of the then popular television show, *The People's Court*, with Michelle acting as the judge.

The video reveals 10-year old Michelle as she is now, an amazing planner, organizer and fun loving leader."

## A FATHER'S PERSPECTIVE

Growing up (and to this day), Michelle was a super athlete, a straight A student, valedictorian at school, a leader and popular.

*"People have always, and still do naturally gravitate toward Michelle. She has an incredible joy that she brings to life. She has a smile that provides light in a large auditorium."*—**Andrew Jezycki**

Michelle's father takes time to reflect on the characteristics and qualities that make his daughter uniquely "Michelle." Qualities that make her stand out and succeed are her attitude and the fact that she: starts with 'we can'; keeps her eye on the prize; focuses on solutions; and, remains open to possibilities.

Even though she may have a pretty clear idea of what needs to happen for someone to accomplish their goal, she wants them engaged and taking ownership. Michelle can envision the end result; she sees what is possible even before she gets involved. But, she lets people work their way through it and then provides guidance when they need it. She gives people latitude to pick "how" to move forward in their own way. Yet, she does not let them stray too far from their goal. "That's why she does a great job as a counselor and as a coach."

"She gets involved with people. She brings her joy to her work and to her relationships. It's contagious. Her way of working with people is to start by saying "we can do this—it's all good.""

Michelle approaches the future with optimism.

According to her father, when Michelle encounters problems, she's certain there are opportunities within them.

"We tried to build in, consciously tried to build in, some excitement and a sense of wonderment or appreciation for this business of life which we're involved. We tried to expose our kids to all sorts of things growing up. We'd go on adventures. Early in the morning on the weekends, everyone would load into the station wagon and just head out to experience the day. There was no particular destination beyond being together and having an adventure. Our goal as parents was to create a sense of wonder and excitement."

"Michelle's got that sense of excitement and wonderment in spades." Michelle's passion and leadership goes beyond achieving for achievement's sake. Michelle truly loves seeing others succeed and reach their goals and dreams. People who know Michelle know her motto: "It's all good. Todo Bien." It is indeed.

## VALUES THAT SHAPE AND GUIDE

*"The influence of one's parents is powerful and permanent."*—**Faye Wattleton**

When asked what values guide her, what her "north star" is and which principles are "nonnegotiable" in life, Michelle responds: "hard work and integrity." Both of which she learned from her parents.

Michelle's parents immigrated to the United States when they were young adults. She saw them rely heavily on their faith and their own values. Her father was a teacher and later principal in the Washoe County School District. During this time she saw her mom working and running three ski shops at Lake Tahoe—while also raising a family. At that time, ski shops required people to spend long periods of time working on their knees in order to help people step into a ski boot, then onto a bench, where you would work at eye level with the boot to make sure it fit and was safe. It was a very physical job, requiring dexterity. It took hand strength and body strength. Michelle's mom did that year after year after year. She didn't complain about it or give the tasks away to someone younger to do. "She'd just rather do it herself."

That example of work ethic and watching both her parents act with integrity impacted her deeply. "I think the values of honesty and being true, not only to other people but to yourself are central."

Andrew and Diana Jezycki came to the U.S. as informed, young individuals. "Our kids could tell that our world view was somehow different than most of the other folks with whom they came in contact. We have a different slant on life and I think it probably did influence our kids growing up."

Her father describes some of the key values he and Diana tried to pass on to their kids:

**"Family** speaks to the importance of valuing and caring for family. No matter what else is going on, family is the center. We emphasized the importance and awareness of the family, both our immediate family of five girls and the extended family.

**Honesty and Kindness** speak to telling the truth and maintaining integrity while at the same time being thoughtful, generous, and considerate when dealing with others.

**Communication and Understanding** speak to need to be open to others, the ambiguities of language and that there are often several levels of meaning when people speak. At the Jezycki house the door was always open. We would host meetings and often Diana or I would be translating from our native languages into English. The look of puzzlement on the kids' faces letting us know that our translation was not quite the meaning that we had intended. The kids still poke fun at my wife's accent to this day. However, there is more tolerance in our family for the ambiguities of language.

**Respect for Self, Others and Nature** speaks to holding yourself in esteem and believing you are worthy of being treated well. It also speaks to going out of one's way to help someone else who one might not even know. All of our girls have traveled to Poland with us. They have experienced and been moved by the respect that the Polish people have toward the land and one another. They experienced first-hand the respect shown to them the as owners of one restaurant kept the doors open past closing and fired up the kitchen, just to save our family the inconvenience of having to go in search of somewhere else to eat. The respect afforded the girls from people they had only just met, served as powerful reminders of the lesson being taught at home about accepting and appreciating others and their differences. It also served to encourage them to engage in conduct worthy of self-respect and to refuse to accept disrespect from others."

*"Self-control is the chief element in self-respect, and self-respect is the chief element in courage."*
—**Thucydides**, *History of the Peloponnesian War*

## FOLLOWING IN HER PARENTS' FOOTSTEPS — CREATING COMMUNITY

In the cul de sac where they live in DC, the neighbors—like most everyone in DC, used to keep to themselves. One by one, Michelle has reached out to get to know people by inviting them to their home. Now, there are regular get-togethers, social events, happy hours, and holiday parties. There are families in six houses, in particular, that all know each other and socialize because of Michelle creating community. She did it again when she moved to Lake Tahoe. After only six months living in the new location, they now have a large circle of very good, caring friends—a Tahoe community.

## INTEGRITY AND WORK ETHIC HAVE BEEN KEY

*"Integrity is doing the right thing, even when no one is watching."*—C. S. Lewis

Michelle has drawn on these values of work ethic and integrity when facing her own challenges at work or in physical training. They allowed her to take the "long view" when dealing with difficult human resource challenges at the U.S. Senate, which often involved partisanship or bias due to political party affiliation. Strong communication skills and integrity have allowed her to take a step back, slow the process down, make sure to leave politics aside, and focus only on the issue at hand.

Her work ethic has helped her stay with a task until it is complete or until a resolution is reached. Then she evaluates whether she should stay the course or change directions.

How does Michelle know when it's time to change direction? Whether she should leave a job, a project, or a client?

"It's about adding value. As long as you're able to add value, you continue. You stay until the job that you were hired to do is either done or now assumed and being performed well by the person you've trained to do it. Then you slowly back out of it."

## COURAGEOUS ENOUGH TO TRY: COURAGE, PREPARATION AND ACTION

*"Your time is limited, so don't waste it living someone else's life. Don't be trapped by dogma—which is living with the results of other people's thinking. Don't let the noise of others' opinions drown out your own inner voice. And most important, have the courage to follow your heart and intuition."*
—Steve Jobs

When people describe Michelle, the words they frequently use are courageous, fearless, giving, smart, loving, caring, adventurous, confident, responsible and learning-driven.

Which got Michelle wondering, "Where did that come from? Where did that gumption come from?"

A brief conversation took place one Sunday morning between Michelle and her partner, Marian, after Marian had described her as courageous.

Michelle to Marian: "Courageous? Me?"

Marian: "Yeah, I never would have the gumption to get behind the helm of a 32 ton, 53 foot yacht and just think I could skipper it."

That made Michelle laugh. "I never thought I couldn't."

Part of it comes from her own life experience. And part of it she attributes to her upbringing and having two immigrant parents. "They showed me a work ethic that nearly scared me because it was so, so solid, so encompassing." Through them, Michelle inherited and adopted the idea that there's really nothing that you can't do. When you get stuck, there are others who can help you out. People ready to assist. "You can call for 'back up' in so many different ways."

When faced with a new challenge, she starts by learning and then getting the coaching and support she needs. The following story exemplifies how Michelle moves through life.

Shortly after purchasing that 53-foot, 32-ton yacht, Michelle wanted to take it out of the harbor. Although an experienced boater, the new vessel was more than double the length of their other boat, and more complex to captain. She found an online simulator program and studied and practiced handling the boat using that. She learned about its engines and operations. She was ready to set out.

She and Marian arrived at the marina for a four-hour lesson and orientation with a very experienced captain. They did a walk-through and Michelle shared with the captain what she learned online. He put her behind the controls and they headed out of the harbor.

"Michelle is fearless. She takes control of the helm and four hours later we come back. She pulled into the slip. No problem. We tie down. We had had a four hour lesson. I don't think the captain even touched the controls once the entire time."

Michelle's reaction? "Let's do it again!"

The conversation went something like this, Michelle to Marian: "We're going out."

Marian, "We as in who?" "Well, you and me."

"What? We need a crew, are you kidding me?" Marian is used to the small boats. She's used to pulling into the dock, stepping off the boat and tying the line.

This yacht is 53 feet long. Marian can't get from the front to the back that fast. She doesn't yet know how to quickly tie these types of lines. "What if something happens?"

"What's going to happen?"

"Well, we could hit another boat and it will cost a lot of money. We could sink this boat. We could die." All of those worries are long shots but each *could* happen.

"We're here. I have to get in practice."

And so it went, back and forth. The next day they went out. No sweat getting out of the slip.

There's an audience of experienced boaters watching two "chicks" maneuver the obviously new boat. They were just waiting for disaster.

"We pull out and Michelle's motoring forward. All the guys are high-fiving. We move down the channel, everything is going fine."

That's when they had a problem getting power. Rather than panicking, Michelle continued under the power used to get out of the marina. They were going slow. Sail boats were passing them by.

Marian suggested calling the captain or someone else for help. Instead, she pulled out the manual and together with Michelle started troubleshooting. They weren't in any danger; they were just out in the

Chesapeake Bay coasting. They were just about ready to head back to the marina when Michelle figured out the problem. It was something simple she'd overlooked on her first time as a solo captain. She'd been working with the adjusters on the small engines to get out of the dock and into the channel. She checked to make sure the engines were synched . . . they were. Then she realized that the main engines were still in neutral. Once she put it in gear, it was full speed ahead and back out into the Chesapeake Bay.

"She was so proud of herself that she figured it out. We came back and she's high-fiving and just feeling so good and so self-assured. To have the gumption to take a boat that size out after only a four hour lesson? That's fearless. That's confidence. That's what life with Michelle is like."

For Michelle, there is no way to experience life or have a meaningful impact without doing all you can. You set a goal, learn what it takes, and start in that direction.

Michelle's father agrees. "For as far back as I can recall she's always been willing to take a risk, willing to step up, step forward." In high school she tried all the sports. She was a good student. She ran for student body office. She was the senior class president. "Michelle was willing to put herself on the line and without any real ego."

In school she looked first to understand what would be required—the general "job description." Then she would decide whether she could do it better than some of the other people who were involved. If yes, she jumped "all in."

"There's a certain awareness and insight that serves as a source of Michelle's confidence. She looks at issues and problems. She becomes aware that she has a role she can play in that situation. Often she holds an even bigger vision of what might be possible through her commitment, involvement or intervention. And she acts."

"There was a man Michelle met in church. He was alone and in poor health. Michelle recognized he was malnourished and had other issues that were not being taken care of. She decided that by intervening, she could make his life better. That there could be an opportunity for this person to be more fully engaged and benefiting from the life that he was living—just by her caring. So Michelle would meet this gentleman for breakfast or lunch after church. She connected him with medical services, where he received a hearing aid. He would say, "Oh, that's what it sounds like [when you can hear]."

Michelle's father remembers the time when Michelle worked for the school district as a truant officer. While school police or other truant officers might "pound their chests" to assert their power in making kids go to school, Michelle would take a different approach: she would take the kid out to breakfast.

"For Michelle it was never a contest of wills. She understood that there were bigger questions that needed to be answered. Questions she could not answer without knowing a kid better. Questions like, 'How do we get this kid to go to school? How do we get this kid to drop the knife that he's got in his hand?' Answers to these questions would lead to information that then would lead to solutions."

## LESSONS FROM HARDSHIP

*"I truly believe that everything that we do and everyone that we meet is put in our path for a purpose. There are no accidents; we're all teachers—if we're willing to pay attention to the lessons we learn, trust our positive instincts and not be afraid to take risks or wait for some miracle to come knocking at our door."*—**Marla Gibbs**

### Make It Matter

Maurice was another kid whose life really touched Michelle during her time as a truant officer. Lately, Maurice had been frequently missing school. Again, Michelle set out to understand why he wasn't attending and see how she could help. It wasn't that Maurice didn't want to go to school. The challenge was getting there.

Like the other kids Michelle worked with, Maurice didn't have many resources. Where other kids might have been able to walk to school, use public transportation, or even ride a bike if they had one, Maurice was at a disadvantage. His battle with cancer had claimed one of his legs, leaving him to maneuver on a steel leg.

Here was a kid who had every reason to say, "Forget it. I'm not going to go to school. I'm not going to put in all this time. My time is limited."

But he didn't. The one thing that really mattered to Maurice was getting a ride so he *could go* to school.

Michelle worked with the school district to make this happen. The day they were finally able to provide him transportation was amazing. Michelle saw Maurice come downstairs in tears saying that he "was the closest to heaven he'd ever been." Michelle had made a difference by caring and going the extra mile for a young man who was dying.

## Success Is Not Always Immediate

*"Never, never be afraid to do what's right, especially if the well-being of a person or animal is at stake. Society's punishments are small compared to the wounds we inflict on our soul when we look the other way."*
—**Martin Luther King, Jr.**

In another case, Michelle was sent to find out why Joe was missing school. Michelle was advised that Joe was a troubled kid and considered 'bad news.' Michelle arrived at Joe's address—a weekly motel on 4th Street. Michelle knocked and Joe answered the door. He was a big kid, already standing 6'2" as a sophomore. He appeared pretty intimidating. Michelle is not tall, or big, or intimidating.

Joe was being bused from a lower economic area of the community as part of integration to attend high school in an upper class neighborhood. The economic disparity between faculty and most of the other students was obvious. Driving into the school's faculty parking lot you would see compact and mid-size sedans; while the student parking lot contained high-end luxury vehicles.

Joe didn't have a car. In fact, he only had one pair of pants and those had a slice on the right cheek. Joe wore a white t-shirt and a large flannel button down shirt to cover the slice.

In Michelle's eyes Joe wasn't a bad kid. He just needed assistance. His mom was working as a waitress during the day and then turning tricks at night; all to keep a roof over their heads. She would come home from the restaurant, wake Joe and send him out of the motel room. He would hang out nearby on the train tracks while she "conducted business."

Then she would call him back in when it was okay to return.

But that wasn't the reason Joe didn't attend school consistently. Joe only made it to school once a week—twice on a good week. He didn't want people to know that he only had one set of clothing. He reasoned that if the students and teachers only saw him every few days they wouldn't notice he always wore the same thing.

For Michelle, this was one of those situations where she had to stand back so she could see the big picture. She had to go beyond what her job required. "Here's a kid who needed clothing. He didn't even have food in this little motel room. He wanted to go to school. The issue wasn't truancy, it was basic needs."

Michelle went to the store and purchased a case of Cup of Noodles. It was not the most nutritious option, but at least it was something that Joe could cook for himself easily. When Michelle went back to check on Joe and see how he was doing, she found someone else had eaten the food she'd purchased for Joe. But, she didn't give up.

"We had to find other ways around Joe's situation." Michelle believed Joe's lack of basic needs (food, clothing, and shelter) coupled with the expectations placed on him by the education and social services systems were unrealistic given his circumstances. It seemed illogical to her.

Michelle continued to visit Joe and show her support. She encouraged him to stay focused on his education even though the other adults in his life did not. She remained a caring adult that believed in him. "I remember at times being scared that I would show up at the motel and be met with aggression on the part of the adults." She expected they would challenge her and demand answers to questions like, "Who do you think you are? I never graduated school, why should he?" She continued to visit.

A couple years later Michelle received a graduation announcement from Joe. "That was like a million bucks to me. To see that not only was he able to make it but he reached back to say, 'Hey, come to this. This is a very important part of my life and you helped me in a small way to piece it all together.'"

"That was huge."

### Failure to Communicate Can Have Grave Consequences

*"The single biggest problem in communication is the illusion that it has taken place."*
**—George Bernard Shaw**

During her time as a truant officer, Michelle also met Linda. Linda was one of those typical "at risk" kids that every agency in the valley knew a little bit about. "Everyone had a hand in the 'cookie jar' of Linda's so-called life." Each person was working in their own field, using their agencies' processes and protocols; and, all with the shared goal of helping Linda. Michelle's job was to find out why Linda wasn't in school and to get her back on track. She approached her work with Linda like she had other kids. But, Linda did not return to school.

Instead, Linda turned up dead in a weekly motel off 2nd Street in Reno, where she lived "on the edge" with others who were just trying to get by. It didn't matter that all of these agencies knew who Linda was or that they were trying to help her. Linda didn't make it. Michelle was crushed.

"I felt like we had all failed. How could this have happened? A young kid was dead even though we had all of the agencies involved, including my own. Yet, it hadn't made a difference. That experience basically rocked my world." It made Michelle even more committed to connecting all the people involved in resolving a situation and ensuring effective communication is taking place. Without real communication, lasting solutions aren't possible.

# THE RIPPLE EFFECTS OF LINDA, JOE AND MAURICE

*"It takes courage to grow up and be who you really are."*—E. E. Cummings

These are just three of the many youth that had an impact on Michelle. They helped her grow up to become more fully who she is today. From them—and other youth—Michelle learned some basic lessons that she takes with her everywhere.

*Linda* met with such a tragic ending; a young girl murdered at a young age. "She died far too soon and that really shook me at the core in terms of the systems that are supposed to help." It caused Michelle to ask herself, "What are we doing? We have all these programs that we are running, and still kids are dying."

*Maurice* showed Michelle that even something seemingly small to one person (a ride) can be "the closest thing to heaven" for another.

From *Joe*, Michelle learned about one kid's reality bumping up against the system and societal expectations. She learned how important it is to take time to understand the context of a person's life, to learn what that person is going through, to understand their needs and challenges. Unless that occurs, it is easy to create a solution disconnected from the real issue. "Can we really have the same level of expectations for each person?

This isn't about expecting less. It's about meeting people where they are. You can't do a 'one size fits all' approach; whether you're dealing with a truant youth, or you're putting together packages for people who've been raped, or you're dealing with someone's livelihood and managing human capital. There are unique circumstances that everybody has whether they share them readily or not."

It's necessary to take each person as they are. "This does not mean you should bend the rules for everybody—but you might alter your approach and better your understanding of how best to help people through certain circumstances if you can remember that everyone is different. If *I* can remember that."

## HELPING OTHERS ACHIEVE PERSONAL GOALS

*"It is an amazing thing to watch someone's personal transformation unfold."*—**Michelle Jezycki**

Michelle helps hundreds exceed their own expectations of physical abilities and health. A few of these people—Alan, Jon, Bonnie, Marian and myself are grateful she did.

## Michelle, Me and a 100-Mile Bike Ride

Michelle gets people to do stuff. You don't even know you're doing it until you've already started it and you're thinking 'Okay, here we go!'

In the end you are glad you did. You stretched. You had fun. You were a little uncomfortable, but you succeeded. You did something you likely would not have without Michelle's prompting and support.

That's how Sarah ended up on a hundred mile bike ride. Michelle asks, "What are you doing next weekend?"

"Nothing." (The opening.)

Michelle again, "Do you have a bike?" (Assessing available resources.)

"Yes, but I haven't been on it in a long time. I'm not sure it's working."

(Barrier #1 offered.)

"Well, let me tune it up for you. We're just going over the hill to a bike ride. The Sacramento Century." (Barrier overcome.)

"Let's register." (Michelle's momentum and commitment builder.)

"Well, I'm not in shape." (Barrier #2 offered.)

"Don't worry. It's not that big of a deal. It's flat, they'll feed us and make sure we have water. It's not really a race for us. We'll do the slow, flat, easy one." (Barrier #2 countered.)

"Well then, OK" (Sarah's in.)

It wasn't until that 11th hour that she actually realized what Michelle had signed them up to do. "I remember getting to the race and thinking "What the—?" These were serious cyclists who were intent on riding a good race. They weren't out for an easy or slow ride.

"Michelle reminded me we were just going to take it easy. Then it was time to start. It was fun. It was everything Michelle said it would be. And, in the end I could say I'd done it and enjoyed it. Because Michelle offered a challenge and I said yes, I now had one more life success under my belt.

## MARIAN

*"Never pass up an opportunity to cheer someone on. You may be just what they need."*—**Michelle Jezycki**

Michelle found she had time on her hands in the evenings when her partner, Marian Huish was working long days as a consultant for a global network of professional firms. She decided to accomplish two goals: complete her Master's in Public Administration, and compete in a 5k run.

Michelle started training and competing. After succeeding in 5k races, she continued her training and upped the ante—longer races, triathlons, marathons. Her dedication and action were encouragement.

Marian, who up until then had seen herself as supporting Michelle was no longer content to just go and watch. After she had been to a few races, she looked at her body, at her long legs and said, "You're healthy. You have two legs." Not everyone competing did. There were amputees, people who were heavier, older, or had some kind of physical impairment that Marian didn't have. They were racing and succeeding.

She asked herself what her excuse was. Why was she standing on the sidelines? That's when she got into the action.

If Michelle hadn't started running and racing, if Marian hadn't been around her during training and daily living, Marian wouldn't have started running or racing too. But she did and now many years later she continues to compete, having recently completed the 2016 Lavaman Waikoloa race on the Big Island of Hawaii.

For Marian training is the challenge. She loves the race, the competition, but not the training and preparation. Working out is not at the top of her "priority list." Michelle serves as a daily motivational "nudge" that helps fuel her commitment to running.

"Every morning Michelle reviews her list of what she's going to accomplish that day. She has a focus and a plan. Then, she'll look at me and ask, 'And you?' She motivates me to work out even when she's not here."

Michelle cheers on everyone's success.

Often when Michelle has finished a race and is driving away, she'll be seen with her head out the window, whistling and carrying on. Encouraging the last racers, the people who are walking the last distances, by shouting: "You've got it! Forward motion!"

## ALAN

### Alan Meets Michelle

> *"Argue for your limitations and they are yours."*
> **—Richard Bach**

Alan Furmin and Michelle met at work. They both worked for the Secretary of the U.S. Senate. The Secretary is basically the chief administrative office of the Senate. There are several departments and several hundred people who work with the Secretary. Alan was the Senate's Parliamentarian and Michelle was hired as the Director of Human Resources for the Office of the Secretary. While not much caring for the administrators in general, Alan liked Michelle.

Alan did his job well. He took care of his people. And, while his responsibilities were substantial, he never liked to be managed. Even though he didn't care for people who did human resource management, Alan found Michelle to be a breath of fresh air and a very sensible human being.

He saw that Michelle was someone that was truly trying to find the best way to have people be productive on the job, and doing that in a positive way. His basic impression of Michelle was that "this is a good person doing the hard job."

One random day, that impression was altered in a way that ultimately changed Alan's life.

Alan's office was in the Capital, while Michelle's office was in a different Senate office building. Alan did not often stray much from the Capital.

Like hundreds of thousands of other Americans, Alan had a weight problem. He would lose some weight, then gain it back again. This particular year Alan had committed to losing some weight and so he tried to get out of his office and walk during his lunch hour. This would allow him to get a more nutritious lunch than what he could get at the Capital. This particular day in the cafeteria, he ran into Michelle who was surprised to see him away from the Capital.

She noticed that he was eating a nutritious lunch. She also noticed that he'd been losing weight. And so, they chatted about Alan's weight loss, personal improvement, and general physical fitness.

It wasn't unusual for Michelle to notice successes. Many people would stop by her office to chat or just approach her in the hallways. They recognized she worked out and that fitness mattered to her. They saw she was helping others achieve success. Some people would ask advice about their own fitness goals. "Can you help me lose weight?" Although not in her "job description" or contract, Michelle would always say yes.

So, when Alan asked if Michelle could help, of course she said yes.

At first they talked about nutrition and how he was progressing. They started with brief chats about his progress. Then Michelle asked, "Have you considered biking?" Later Michelle shared that she was just beginning to work out in preparation for a triathlon. Alan was impressed. He'd never considered anything of that nature a possibility for himself.

The door to Alan's future opened just a bit, as Michelle continued, "Well you know, I was a casual jogger." She went on to say she was training for an entry level triathlon at the Bethesda Chevy-Chase YMCA. That was Alan's neighborhood. The door opened a bit wider. Michelle asked, "Why don't I come up to your house, and we'll take a look at the triathlon course together?"

The next weekend they went for a bike ride together. Alan was like a kid who just got the training wheels off his first bike. He didn't stop smiling and at the end of the ride stated he hadn't thought he could do a ride like that.

After that, Michelle would run and Alan would cheer her on through her training.

Then the day of the sprint triathlon arrived. As Michelle crossed the finish line, she looked at Alan and said, "Next year, you do it."

"Huh?"

Michelle countered, "Why not? Why not you? I could do it. Everybody can do things if they set goals and work toward them."

It never occurred to Alan to do the local triathlon. He was a casual jogger. He rode a bicycle when he was younger. He considered himself a terrible swimmer.

"Can't" Does Not Exist

Alan's answers to Michelle's "Why not?" questions were stated as reasons he could not.

"Well, I don't have a bicycle." No problem. Michelle loaned him one of hers. Excuse number one gone.

"I'm a terrible swimmer." Michelle countered, "Well you have a year to train. We can work on it. Get in the pool and swim. No excuse."

"I don't run very fast, anyway." "Then, begin running. Just start where you are."

And, that's what happened. There were no acceptable excuses as to why Alan could not race.

*"Whether you think you can, or think you can't, you're right."*—Henry Ford

Alan took from Michelle the understanding that there are things out there that you may or may not think you can do. But until you try, you honestly can't know if you can succeed. So why not try? Why not do a little more than you think you're capable of doing? That's how Alan got started.

The next year they competed in the triathlon together.

## Looking Back

It was in 2004 when they ran into each other at the cafeteria, the same year Michelle competed in her first sprint triathlon; and just one year later, Alan competed in his first (of four) triathlon events. It's the biking that he loved the most and so he continued to do that for exercise. Now more than ten years later, Alan has biked fifteen thousand miles, traveling between 1,200 and 1,500 miles per year. Biking has become his "go-to" means of exercise. He has lost more than 80 pounds and he's more fit at 65 than he was in his forties. His wife declared Michelle had helped 'bring her husband back.' Michelle credits Alan, saying he did all the work. Michelle started the ball rolling and then continued to encourage him to challenge himself. But it was Alan that succeeded.

"These are the ripple effects of what Michelle had started with me. I remained physically active at a time when guys my age are becoming less likely to." As Alan reflects looking at his life, he realizes the thousands of miles he's now ridden are a direct result from a casual conversation with Michelle at the cafeteria. All because she noticed that he had been losing weight and struck up a conversation to support his efforts. In turn, he is having his own ripple effect. He has been an inspiration to friends who now ride hundreds of miles each year.

"It's ironic. My dedication to riding has made me an easier person to deal with. It gives me an outlet. I just flat out enjoy jumping on my bike and exploring our local area. I go places I wouldn't have otherwise gone. All as a result of this [change]."

What lead to Alan's transformation? Was it Michelle engaging Alan in a conversation? Was it Alan's readiness to connect and talk about health? Was it something else? If Alan hadn't already made a decision and taken (literally) steps toward achieving his goals and losing weight, would he have been open to Michelle's suggestion that he show her the triathlon course? If Alan hadn't started down that road of wanting to get healthier and get out of his office to walk, would he have been someone Michelle noticed or engaged with?

According to Alan, taking action on his part was necessary to show his desire. He believes Michelle will work with somebody who is willing to work with themselves . . . people who are inclined to better themselves. "If you are willing to put in the work, she's more than willing to help with that."

It's been more than a decade since Alan completed that triathlon. Now all these years later, what advice would Alan offer to someone who is where he was ten years ago? Someone with a goal or dream and not sure how to get there; someone that might not have his good fortune to run into Michelle or someone like her?

Easy.

"Don't sell yourself short. Just try to do a little more, and then do a little more still. Look for a little bit of improvement, at whatever age. If you don't try, obviously, you're not going to succeed. There's a tremendous amount of satisfaction in each little incremental step."

"People see you accomplish something and one part of their brain thinks 'I wonder if *I* could even do a *piece of that* [accomplishment]?'Then there are those who have enough courage to ask for help."

Whenever Michelle sees someone taking the first step, she offers encouragement. She notices people lacing up their shoes, taking a walk or eating healthy. That's the opportunity to reinforce the behavior and habit with a "That's great!" "Good for you!" She knows that acknowledgment and relationships open the door for a whole other, deeper conversation that can lead to change.

"Michelle is more than willing to show you where the first step is and how far that first step can take you. She just has the best attitude of anybody I know. She starts with where people are, and says 'let's just step it up a notch.'"

> **"A person doesn't necessarily have to know where the steps will lead. She just wants you to take the next one."**
> **—Alan Furmin**

## IRONMAN JON

Michelle's friend "Ironman Jon" Callahan is another perfect example of what someone with a burning desire can achieve when they meet someone that actively supports them. At 45 years old, Jon had a dream of running a triathlon. As someone with Downs

Syndrome, his abilities would often be discounted and underestimated. But, not by Michelle. Jon would drop by Michelle's office at the Senate and share his dreams with her, and she would encourage him.

"What I learned from working with Jon was that nothing is impossible, regardless of if you have Downs or whether you have other conditions, issues or obstacles in your life, there's no reason not to put one foot in front of the next and accomplish your goals."

Michelle started working with Jon. She accompanied him on runs and swims; helping him move closer and closer to his goal. One day when Jon and Alan Furmin were both in Michelle's office, the conversation turned to triathlons. Jon looked at Alan and said, "next year, you do this [triathlon] with me."

Alan just replied "okay." He couldn't very well say no—especially since Jon, now known as "Ironman Jon," had challenges that Alan didn't.

Jon successfully completed his triathlon. His mom, Adelina Callahan credits Michelle for putting joy into Jon's life.

## MORE RIPPLES—NO MORE SIDELINES

*"The most effective way to do it is to do it."*
**—Amelia Earhart**

## Exceeding Your Own Expectations—Armando

Then there's Michelle's friend, Armando Loranko. At 63 he was out of shape and overweight. He loved his food and wine. He thought people who ran marathons were "crazy people," but he was intrigued. He would see Michelle come back from her training workouts and just shake his head.

Then one day Michelle saw that there was a half marathon planned for Portugal that would go through Armando's home town of Lisbon; a town where his mother still lived. Michelle handed Armando a brochure and he did what she predicted he would: he went to Google Earth to look at the route map. The race would go directly by his mom's house. He knew the bridge it would be crossing. He saw the route in his head.

He asked Michelle, "Are you going to run this race?" "I don't know, Armando. Are you?"

"What? I am not a runner. I've never run anything."

Michelle simply asked, "Well then, when are you going to get started?"

With six months to train and the enticement of Michelle's coaching and support, Armando went all in. He decided it was his opportunity to show himself that he could really do it. He started slow. He was out of breath. He had no idea how out of shape he was, but he stayed with it. Within one month he began feeling better.

When the time came, Armando, his wife, Michelle and Marian flew to Portugal for the half marathon. Michelle ran alongside Armando from start to finish, while Marian ran ahead to capture Armando's success in photos. He crossed the bridge he knew from his youth. He ran past his mom's house—his family and friends. And he proved to himself what he could accomplish when he set his sights on a goal and then went after it.

Armando's success caused a ripple effect in his own life. He started training for a *full* marathon with his eyes on an upcoming race in Portugal. He knew he could do it. "The clearest benefit that I got, was I lost weight without even trying."

Who knows how many others were inspired because Armando stepped up and committed to his goal.

Michelle asserts: "No matter if you're in your 40's, 50's, or 60's . . . If you are overweight, big boned, have low self-esteem. Whatever the issue might be, you can change that, put a dent in it. And, you can also transform your life."

### Staying Committed—Bonnie

Bonnie Knight wanted to lose weight. She'd been working out for nearly two years and had lost 50 pounds. She was clearly someone pursuing a goal. But she'd hit a plateau and wasn't breaking through, even with her dedication to losing weight and getting healthy. Then she met Michelle and a new challenge was offered. "Have you ever thought of running?" Bonnie had her self-doubts. She wasn't a runner. When she shared the idea with others, the people around her expressed their doubts. They didn't think she could do it. They were sure her knees and ankles would not be strong enough due to her excess weight.

So if she had doubts and others did too, then it seemed there wasn't a point in even trying. But the idea of running had sparked a desire and the desire began to grow stronger.

Michelle encouraged her, just like she does everyone.

*"You don't need to see the whole staircase, you just need to take the first step."*—**Michelle Jezycki**

So, Bonnie started slow. She started by walking two minutes then jogged one minute. She continued to progress from there. She did not listen to those who doubted her ability or eventual success. She focused on making small improvements every day. She saw herself making gains and achieving results. She persevered and finally entered her first competition: a 5K race, which she easily completed.

Now when Bonnie looks back and thinks of Michelle, she recalls that first race and the process of training and working with Michelle. "It changed how I thought about myself. It just changed everything."

Michelle credits Bonnie with her own success. "It's a byproduct of looking after yourself. Making that change internally; which is now exposing itself externally."

## STAYING THE COURSE: WHAT RACING MEANS TO MICHELLE

*"How many times in life do we get an opportunity to practice being uncomfortable? To know we have the resources to succeed but it will require commitment."*
—**Michelle Jezycki**

People have told Michelle her racing is extreme. But, to her it's an opportunity to practice being uncomfortable and pushing through. It's her path to knowing what she's capable of doing and achieving. Michelle sees racing as a chance to practice, to know, and to develop herself on a deeper level.

"How many times in life do we get an opportunity to practice being uncomfortable; to know we have the resources to succeed but it will require commitment? Yet, if we push on—work mile after mile—we can and will get to our end result"

There are many times in racing where it gets difficult; where it would just be easier to quit. This is the same in life. There are times when people want to bail, want to quit, and even question themselves about the goal they've set, the path they are on. They may even say, "Oh my God, what was I thinking?"

For Michelle, these are the exact moments in life (and racing) that fill her reservoir. When she gets into difficult situations, when she finds herself asking, "How am I going to get through this?" she sits back and dips into the reservoir she's built from pushing through previous challenges and obstacles, from staying the course and taking one step after another. When it gets difficult she reminds herself:

"There's nothing I can't get through. I've practiced for these situations. I've faced uncertainty and fear and I have succeeded." It's all about taking the next step even in the face of uncertainty.

Many people who meet Michelle may mistakenly think life has been easy for her, even carefree. That her drive, energy and enthusiasm have carried her forward effortlessly. That isn't the case. Just like the rest of us, Michelle knows something about fear, uncertainty, and life's challenges.

# STRETCHING INTO THE CHALLENGE

*"Success is due to our stretching to the challenges of life.*
*Failure comes when we shrink from them."*
—**John C. Maxwell**[18]

As a young girl Michelle compared herself to her sisters. She became self-conscious. Her sisters were always thin and beautiful. Every time she would go back for family functions she would notice how they were always made up, with perfect hair and nails. As self-confident as Michelle was, she still didn't want to be compared to her sisters. These were feelings that Michelle has had to deal with over time. While old feelings and past worries contribute to her unceasing drive, it's Michelle's intrinsic spirit and spark that keep the energy moving forward in her commitment to health. Marian shares ". . . all of those things [feelings and past worries] drive Michelle to keep herself looking good and feeling good. Of course, her love for racing motivates her even further. It's all those things combined that keep her healthy."

This became especially important when Michelle was diagnosed with multiple sclerosis (MS). As anyone would imagine it was devastating, especially for someone who is as healthy as an ox. "Most people are diagnosed in their 30s, she was 45 at the time of her diagnosis. I believe that her prolonged diagnosis came as a result of her lifestyle; her healthy eating, her business, all of it."

Such a diagnosis could have sidelined Michelle. Another person may have decided to cut back on enjoying the things that give their life meaning—training, competing, coaching other athletes. But not Michelle.

She and Marian talked about the treatment options and they did their homework. Neither Michelle nor Marian liked prescriptions as a solution, as Marian shared: "We talked to some other people with MS and found out the side effects of the drugs can be worse than the symptoms in many cases. People have awful nightmares, someone said it was like they have a cold all the time. Who wants to feel like that?" Marian redoubled her research efforts and found a doctor from the 1940's who studied MS and the impact of diet on the disease.

"This doctor was really out of the ordinary at that time in history to study the impact of diet on diseases. Of course people dismissed him as a witch doctor. They said he did not know what he was talking about and that his work and studies were unfounded. But he studied hundreds of people in a controlled environment and basically caused them to remove meat from their diets. He demonstrated that people with MS who don't eat meat live longer and the symptoms don't show for many, many years later. He found these changes stop the progression of MS."

That was just enough for Michelle and Marian to change their diets. Michelle has been aggressive, doing everything she can diet-wise to stop the progression of MS. Michelle cut out meat. They don't cook it at home and they don't order it when they go out. Michelle is always watching and doing research into the health benefits of changing diets.

Now, on the flip side, Marian notes Michelle is not cutting back on her workouts. "They say heat and extensive exercise can also make MS progress, but she's not willing to give that up."

While she is still very active, training and competing, Michelle has experienced some issues from the disease. "Even before last summer she had some numbness in her leg and that was impacting her gait running and also swimming. I'm not sure if she'll ever do another Ironman but she'll at least do what she can, she'll certainly swim and if she can, she'll continue to scuba dive. She'll do whatever things she can physically while she's able."

As if the MS wasn't challenge enough, just over a year ago Michelle tore her ACL as she and Marian were doing a favor and taking a friend of a friend out skiing. Michelle is an expert skier, but that didn't save her from tearing her ACL as they finished the day in less than optimal ski conditions. The orthopedic surgeon said it would take 4–6 weeks for the swelling to subside before he could operate. Recuperation would take another nine months—maybe a year, even with physical therapy.

In typical Michelle fashion, she learned what she could do herself to help the healing begin and get the swelling down. So, in the middle of winter, when most people are trying to stay warm and dry, Michelle would go to a nearby beach and wade carefully into the icy cold water of Lake Tahoe. At home, she would use ice and transcutaneous electric nerve stimulation (TENS). Her efforts paid off. She was ready for surgery long before predicted. Post-surgery she continued following the instructions of her physical therapists and doing everything on her own to support and advance the healing. Only a few months post-surgery she was given clearance to participate in a swim event in Lake Tahoe, on the condition that she not use her injured leg. This meant training to swim with only one leg. She did it. It's been just over a year now and Michelle is once again skiing and training. In April 2016 she completed in the Lavaman Waikoloa triathlon in Hawaii along with Marian.

Michelle shares her challenges—internal and physical—and also what running and racing has done to help her grow and reach for more in her life. She knows that when people begin to face their fear and uncertainty, to move forward and see progress, and experience "wins" each day, it flows into other areas of their life. It has for her; just as it has for Alan, Jon, Bonnie, Armando, Sarah and Marian.

# CHURCH AND COMMUNITY LEADERSHIP

*"Only a life lived in the service to others is worth living."*—**Albert Einstein**

When Michelle and Marian first met in DC they had different faiths. Michelle had been raised Catholic while Marian was raised Disciple of Christ Protestant. After they had been together a couple of years, it was time to find a church they could both love and share; and, they found one. It wasn't long after joining that Michelle became aware of the opportunity to become a Deacon and within a year she accomplished that honor. Then another opportunity for leadership arose and she became an Elder and was involved in committees and meetings.

Through those relationships, the church learned that Michelle is a human resource expert with a lot of training. The church had personnel and budget challenges. They asked for help and Michelle stepped up. She attended meetings two or three nights per week to help the church's leadership. Due to her expertise, Michelle was asked to handle challenging and potentially litigious issues in a compassionate way. Ultimately, her help saved the church the expense of hiring a consultant or lawyer.

Then Michelle and Marian decided to live on two coasts, and Michelle returned to her roots at Lake Tahoe. They bought a condominium in March and by June of that year had moved in. One of the first things

Michelle wanted to do was to serve on the board of the homeowners association. This is typically the last thing that owners want to do, especially new owners. It's a volunteer role that requires handling a variety of issues which all require a lot of time; time which she didn't have, running two businesses and traveling frequently.

Within a year, Michelle was not only on the association board but was serving as board president. It did consume time. There were phone calls at all hours of the day and night. There were dozens, if not hundreds, of emails each day. Owners were both passionate and vocal about their concerns and complaints. It would have been easy to minimize or ignore them. But instead, Michelle took time to understand. She investigated to learn the facts and the truth of each situation. Then she tried to see it from the homeowner's perspective before attempting to resolve anything. In the end, some tricky and potentially volatile situations were resolved because she was willing to take ownership and responsibility for the larger community of homeowners without judgement or blame.

Marian shares, "Michelle's not afraid to step up and do what needs to be done. She's a problem solver and wants to help people find solutions to their problems. She wants to have impact and make a difference, and so she chooses to lead."

# BEST PIECES OF ADVICE

*"The key to any piece of advice is to remember to use it. You can get all the advice in the world but it doesn't help if you don't actually use it."*—**Michelle Jezycki**

Others' advice has helped Michelle over the years. One of the best pieces of advice Michelle received was that it is okay to think outside the box—even when you are working within a system like a school district or other institution that is less flexible. She learned that it's possible to be empathetic, while also being impactful.

She learned this in her 20's from Joe Anastasio, who was then Washoe County School District's student service director and her boss when she was a truant officer. Michelle describes Joe as a man with a big heart that would show up in surprising situations. He had a strong but fair disciplinary hand. Had it not been for Joe giving Michelle the green light, go-ahead to pull together private resources in order to give help and hope to kids living on the edge, there would've been more dropouts.

Michelle learned that thinking outside the box can preempt failures that occur when systems are "being strangled by their own red tape."

Joe was also the person that opened a door of opportunity and exposure to the national scene for Michelle as part of a regional planning project that eventually lead her to Washington, DC to work on behalf of missing and exploited children and then to direct human resources for the US Senate. When it comes to challenging or difficult situations, the advice Michelle offers others is to not personalize feedback or information, even when it's harsh, or hard to hear. When people say and do things that are difficult, look to extract a piece of the other person's reality. Try to understand what they are seeing, feeling or experiencing.

"Slow down, step back and try to see the other person's experience as if it were your own. You don't have to agree, but you can empathize and acknowledge."

Also important is getting a handle on your emotions. This does not mean people should not have emotions, but it's important to understand them and ensure they do not dictate your actions. Michelle likes to remind folks that by taking a timeout to "check in" with yourself to understand what's really going on, people can avoid creating situations that they later have to repair. "When you're in a leadership position you have to learn to have better control of your emotions. It's an important skill to learn and to practice."

"Instead of questioning the different experiences and paths ahead, it's okay to just allow them in. Even if they seem like crazy detours. Experience life events, take from them what you can, then move onto the next thing."


## SOMEONE DOING SOMETHING AMAZING: MARGEE—AN INSPIRATION FOR MICHELLE FROM ACROSS THE GLOBE

*"Those who say it can't be done should not interrupt those who are doing it."*—George Bernard Shaw

The President of the American University of Nigeria (AUN), Margee Enfign, is someone Michelle looks to as a changemaker. Margee views her role and how she thinks to be far "outside the box" of a typical university president. She seeks to inspire and empower others to go and do more. At AUN the faculty and staff are encouraged to go beyond to contribute to the community. They are feeding the hungry, doing community work, and they are connecting at a personal level—and as a result, staff is starting to come around to Margee's view of education.

One project they've taken on in partnership with the community is called *Waste to Wealth*. The University teaches the community how to take the plastic that is normally burned in piles and convert it into products they can sell, such as place mats, iPhone case covers, and other useful items. They use the profits to improve their own lives.

What amazes Michelle is the fact that Margee could simply focus her efforts on exclusively operating AUN. She could increase enrollment, recruit more people and ensure the educational agenda is fulfilled in order to get young people the best education they can get. They are all important, powerful goals. But, Margee has gone beyond. Because of Margee, AUN is focused on developing a community of which everyone is proud. She's part of a peace initiative in which she started to bring Muslims and Christians together around the same table; men and women. All leaders in their faiths (e.g., bishops and cardinals and other high level people) discussing how together they can make a difference and bring peace to northeast Nigeria.

Margee assumes more responsibility than that of being the president of the university. To some, she seems more like a mayor.

In April 2014, Boko Haram, which translates as "western education is sin," abducted nearly 300 girls as they slept in their rooms at a secondary school for girls in Chibok. This was not the first or last abduction. Boko Haram has forced millions of people from their homes, killed tens of thousands, and abducted hundreds. During the abduction, two of the guards protecting the school were killed. The girls were transported away into the night. In response, the state government closed all secondary schools and sent students home. Only 58 girls have returned to their homes. Most of the others' whereabouts are unknown. But, not all.

Twenty-three of the Chibok girls who escaped are recovering at AUN. A sponsorship program was established to ensure these girls get their education. When it came time to bring the girls from Chibok to AUN, Margee insisted on going and being a part of that convoy.

Michelle begged and pleaded with her to remain behind; reminding her that if something happened to Margee there would be no one to lead the effort.

But in the end, Margee went.

"She's very passionate and she takes the job of university president far outside the typical boundaries."

**Humankind. Be Both.**

Margee's story is one of courage and commitment to her community in Nigeria. That, along with what Michelle has been doing as a consultant to support Margee and the American University of Nigeria, has had an impact on Michelle as well.

*"The real voyage of discovery consists not in seeking new landscapes but in having new eyes."*
**—Marcel Proust**

Michelle now asks us to "imagine what a better world we would be living in if we could all be a bit more compassionate, less "me" centered and practiced kindness on a daily basis, rather than in response to a crisis-based or a season of the year."

Michelle attributes this new effort to a combination of things: "The whole Nigeria connection, traveling back and forth, and seeing how differently they live and with far less than we have. In many ways, many of them look happier than we do. The kids in the U.S. in particular, have their cell phones, their iPads and other electronics, and those things have become their babysitter. There, in Nigeria, they have sticks and dirt. They're joyful. They're amazing individuals, not that the kids here aren't. But it's interesting how that community responded when Boko Haram had attacked Maiduguri.

"All of these internally displaced persons (IDPs) came down—I think a total of 400,000 IDPs—into these little villages. Here are people with nothing, people that lost everything they had, and now they are coming to a community that has nothing itself. That community welcomed them with open arms. I was amazed. They were Christians and Muslims alike. The Christians are at the mosques. The cathedrals and the churches were open for everyone as well. It was really neat. Then, two weeks later I see [U.S.] parents upset that that 1,300 refugees are coming their way, and this [the U.S.] is not a third world country."

That's just one example that frustrated Michelle. When she sees some of the ugliness being spread, whether it's political or racial, like thinking one type of life matters more than another, she reminds people that all human lives matter, regardless of skin color.

Over the years Michelle has impacted people one after another, and those individuals have gone on to touch the lives of others. The ripple effect from her newest endeavor spans the globe. Michelle recently launched a new social give-back organization called Humankind. Be Both®. The organization is committed to getting this message—Humankind. Be Both.—out worldwide. The purpose is to remind us all to "walk the talk," to remember that we are all part of humankind so we should be both human and kind.

*"We're made the same. We produce the same. We bleed the same."*—**Michelle Jezycki**

# CHAPTER 6
# GERARD & STACEY

Gerard Ungerman and Stacey Wear were introduced to me through a colleague who felt their life's work and passion aligned with my goals for sharing what's possible and encouraging people to act.

What is amazing to me about Gerard and Stacey is how they came from two different continents, with very different backgrounds, beliefs and goals in life; yet, their life experiences brought them both to a shared dream. Over the course of their lives, each of them has reached beyond their comfort zones to pivot direction in what that thought they wanted to do, or be when they realized they were heading in the wrong direction. When their hopes and dreams didn't turn out as planned, they simply looked for a new way to contribute to the world. Only this time they would do it together.

## GERARD'S BACKGROUND

Raised in the Northern Normandy area of France, Gerard was a disinterested kid. He grew up angry and ashamed. His own mother was uninvolved and not kind. And, as if that wasn't enough, Gerard also had a miserable time in school. He was bounded by people that criticized, often to extremes. All of his negative experiences contributed to him becoming hardened. As he got older, he continued to struggle to get ahead. Only years later, after reading about the symptoms of Asperger's and the autism spectrum did it occur to him why learning had been so difficult and why he had been so hard on himself.

*"We may never actually meet the people that change our lives. Our role models may never know that's who they are for us."*—**Sarah Boxx**

For Gerard, both were true.

Growing up without a father, he was forever looking for examples of manhood, male role models, and men to emulate. Gerard found a powerful influence in movies and particularly in Clint Eastwood. Eastwood's characters were powerful, rough and very tough men who were simultaneously humane, compassionate, and had common sense. They had a strong moral compass. They were willing to help the underdog; to step in where other men would not. Movies like *Honky Tonk Man* and *Bronco Billy* spoke to Gerard and showed him how men could courageously follow an ideal even if it had consequences. These were men that even if they 'hit the dust' while pursuing a path or trying something different and, they persisted; especially, while trying to help other people.

Gerard could see himself becoming *that* kind of man in his mind.

Like many youth his age, Gerard had an interest in becoming a warrior as a teenager. At the same time, he saw even more clearly through books and movies that there was more to war than meets the eye. Being a warrior was accompanied by tremendous suffering. And, profiteering was involved.

It wasn't only films that influenced Gerard; it was the politics. From a young age, he wanted to know who pulled the strings. Who was it that caused things to happened, especially when it came to instigating war?

After completing secondary school (equivalent of high school and some college), Gerard entered the military academy and he fulfilled his goal of becoming an officer. From the beginning, he thought he would be career military. He had friends who had military careers and some were even stationed in other countries with secure commands. Other friends had become mercenaries.

That might have been Gerard's life too had he not experienced two events that spun his life 180 degrees.

*"Relish everything that's inside of you, the imperfections, the darkness, the richness and light and everything. And that makes for a full life."*
**—Anthony Hopkins**

He was 19 and living at the military academy. On the weekends while the others went home, Gerard remained behind to study. One night he was sound asleep, the next he was having a vision.

He was in a combat zone, on the ground with his back against a wall. Just then he realized that his stomach had been torn open. His skin and muscle shredded by shrapnel, his guts falling freely on his lap. Thick blood, his blood, pooled there. In an instant, he knew he was finished. It was over. His entire life had gone by and he had nothing more than some adventure and violence to show for it. Nothing. Gerard realized in that moment that he had lived for nothing; and now was dying to live. His life had been wasted. His sobbing woke him up.

A week later it happened again. Another vision.

This time he was not asleep. He was alone in his room in total darkness. In the distance a thin light appeared. He stared at it. There was nowhere else to look. It was the only thing besides the darkness. Just a thin light that glowed. This was a different experience than the previous week. The light beckoned him.

He was uncertain. Should he go to it? And then the light came to him. A radiant ball of white light. Pure goodness. It engulfed him. He didn't know what it was but he knew it was good. It kept building in him. He felt its power. The experience of his death followed by his envelopment by the light set him on a new course. He changed overnight.

"I'm doing what I do and I live the way I live today—with no fear, with faith and doing good for the world—all because of this light. It was and is like magic."

When his first contract with the military was up, he left.

When Gerard left the military, films influenced him once again as he experienced the power of documentaries. He was moved by films and videos from the Empowerment Project, co-founded by David Kasper and Barbara Trent in 1984. This included Trent and Kasper's 1989 film "Cover-Up: Behind the Iran Contra Affair," and their 1992 Oscar® winning "The Panama Deception" the untold story of the December 1989 U.S. invasion of Panama.

However, it was Allan Francovich that transformed his sense of what is possible through film and set him on a different course. Among Francovich's many amazing documentaries, "On Company Business,"[19] "The Maltese Double-Cross—Lockerbie" and "Operation Gladio" really stood out. Gerard now saw it was possible to use documentaries to wake up audiences around the world to the reality of international power politics.

Like Eastwood's characters, these film makers' life works had required courage, risk taking and fortitude.

Gerard had first-hand experience with war. He had been in the military during the second Gulf War for Europe (but the first Gulf War for the West) in 1990–91. He found himself incensed when he listened to the news about fighting in Iraq. His anger turned to resolve. One day he would do something to expose the real motives behind the West, the US, and their European/other allies, for going to war in Iraq.

It clicked. It made sense. Gerard was awakened by both the documentaries' content and their form. He stepped into the next phase of his journey: becoming an investigator, a "secret agent" searching for the truth and willing to uncover the dirt behind politics and power. And then, presenting the results in a nicely crafted package, all as a means to communicate more broadly and to say, "Look, this is what's happening and will continue to happen unless we wake up."

Although he now had a direction, he had no idea of how to get there. He proceeded down the path regardless. It would be years later before he would see the result of this resolve bear fruit. He produced a number of documentaries, some edgy and all aimed at revealing information. Films included:

*The Hidden Wars of Desert Storm* (2001), a documentary featuring interviews with Gen. Norman Schwarzkopf, Ramsey Clark, Denis Halliday, Jean

Heller and Scott Ritter; and John Hurt as the narrator.

*Plan Colombia: Cashing In on the Drug War Failure* (2003) a gripping documentary takes an in depth look at the Colombian Drug war and the failed U.S. efforts to make an impact on the trafficking to America.

*The Oil Factor: Behind the War on Terror* (2005 documentary), narrated by Ed Asner, with Noam Chomsky, Richard Heinbert, and others, this film won the Women Film Critics Circle Awards for Courage in Filmmaking.


## STACEY'S BACKGROUND

*"When we try to pick out anything by itself, we find it hitched to everything else in the universe."*
**—John Muir**

The Sacramento River runs right through Redding, in Northern California. You can, on a daily basis see Mount Shasta to the north and Mount Lassen to the east. You are surrounded by foothills and only a few hours from the coast, and trees are everywhere. It's gorgeous. It's where Stacey Wear grew up.

Her family did not have a lot of money, but they always took family vacations. Sometimes it was camping, other times they would travel to visit family in Southern California. At least once a year her father would load everybody into the Ford Station Wagon and they would head south to Los Angeles.

Even as a young girl she could see the impact of urban growth on the natural environment. Driving south from Redding, each mile closer to Southern California highlighted the stark distinctions between the northern and southern parts of California. The north was less populated. It had natural beauty and a variety of outdoor resources; while Southern California had spreading concrete cities and water that came from outside the region.

When her family finally arrived in Southern California each trip, she was reminded again of what not to do when planning a city.

It was overbuilt. There was concrete everywhere. There appeared to be no regard for nature except for the beach, and even there they were building right up to it. Nature became more choked out. Each year when her family returned there was more cement, more growth, more roads, more cars and no end in sight. There was much that detracted from what could be a beautiful place.

The beauty of the natural world had made an early impression on Stacey. The contrast between where she was raised and of the Southern California environment was stark. Stacey began to wonder where it would all end. Questions began to form in her mind: How were all of these people getting water in a place that didn't have water? How could people live and live well in a place where the air is horrible? How could nature survive for the same reasons?

Describing her parents as open-minded, progressive Democrats that raised their children in a fairly traditional Italian Catholic household, she comes by her sense of social justice naturally. Her parents paid attention to politics and what was happening. They were engaged. It all unfolded in front of her, on television, in her home, in school. She saw it all. Even at a very young age she felt compelled by what the college students were doing.

*"One touch of nature makes the whole world kin."*
**—William Shakespeare**

From those beginnings, her motivation for doing good work in the world took root. Her sense of social justice, and a commitment to caring for nature and the planet. Born in California in the early sixties, Stacey grew up during the tumultuous times of the fight for civil rights and the Vietnam War.

She read an historical fiction novel in high school, *Five Smooth Stones* by Ann Fairbairn that set her on a path. The book had been on her mom's bookshelf for years, unnoticed by Stacey. But, one day she picked it up and read the story of an interracial couple who meet at school and fall in love right at the peak of the Civil Rights Movement. All types of terrible things happen to them as a couple, but particularly to David Champlin. David is a black man who had become successful after being born into poverty in Depression-era New Orleans. All of that is forfeited as he becomes a leader in the movement. Fired up at the conclusion of the book, Stacey declared to her mom, "I don't know what I'm going to do, but I'm going to do something." Her fire for social justice was ablaze. She just knew that things should be different.

She set out on her own path, eager to discover more, living a year abroad as an exchange student in Japan. She returned home thinking she would gradually build on her Japanese-speaking skills. She planned on moving and working in San Francisco at the embassy or perhaps a Japanese multinational company.

However, life had other plans as other opportunities opened up before she could move to the city. She returned to Japan to teach English for another year. Then, she moved to Hawaii with her boyfriend, whom she later married. She had her first of two daughters, then she had another.

Life moved on. Yet, she felt she was moving in a direction that didn't seem true to who she was. As she was approaching 40, her marriage broke apart. Her head "exploded" and she realized she had to change her life. Chasing upward mobility, getting a bigger house and other signs of success were not for her. She was disconnected from her true self. Now was her chance to do things differently. She packed up and moved to Chico, California and to a different life.


## STACEY MEETS GERARD

*"They say that there are moments that open up your life like a walnut cracked, that change your point of view so that you never look at things the same way again."*
**—Jodi Picoult**

Stacey started by searching for a job that mattered. A job that had a strong component of giving back. All the better if it paid well, but that wasn't the primary criteria—even though she was now a single mom. The first job she accepted didn't pay well. In fact it didn't pay at all.

She was a volunteer at the community radio station, KZFR. The work mattered. She was engaged and enthusiastic. It brought her in contact with so many different people who had different ideas; each person turning those ideas into specific efforts and actions. These were people who were passionate about what could be. Stacey felt at home and knew she had found her path. It was where she wanted to be.

She felt her life open up in a real way. She was being exposed to so many great people and provocative ideas, while remaining true to herself. She was living authentically, maybe for the first time in her life.

After only a few months, she was hired as the office manager. She was now being paid for doing what she loved and what mattered to her. This is when she met Gerard.

By this point, Gerard had been working for some years as a documentary filmmaker. He was coming through Chico to show one of his films. He was to be Stacey's first ever on-air public affairs interview.

That's how they met. The French-born documentary filmmaker for social justice, and the social justice advocate radio station manager.


## THE SHIFT FROM EXPOSING HORROR TO EXPOSING HOPE

*"Always remember, you have within you the strength, the patience, and the passion to reach for the stars to change the world."*—**Harriet Tubman**

Between 1996 and 2004, and before meeting and working with Stacey, Gerard and his then business partner Audrey Brohy made a number of documentaries—most of which had focused on war: the business of war; the war on drugs; guerrilla warfare in Peru; wars in Iraq and Afghanistan; politics; suffering; and, people caught in the crossfire of one type or another. All were important topics. Some of the films did well; and, some not as well as others.

Gerard was getting burned out. People did not really want to know what was happening. That's when his thinking began to change again. Maybe the path was less about ferreting out secrets and behind the scenes dealings, and more about the stories of people's understandings and finding solutions.

His next project *Belonging*, which he produced in 2008, was different. This film combined a scientific and spiritual journey into humanity's footprint on Earth, with a call to action for use reduction and conservation. The film failed. Perhaps the timing was wrong. No matter the reason, the result was loss: loss of time, management, and finance. Gerard's resolved not to make another documentary.

## RESPECTFUL REVOLUTION IS BORN

*"As you navigate through the rest of your life, be open to collaboration. Other people and other people's ideas are often better than your own. Find a group of people who challenge and inspire you, spend a lot of time with them, and it will change your life."*
—**Amy Poehler**

From the first time they spoke during an on air radio interview, Gerard believed the seed of their relationship was planted; that on a soul level their connection was instant. Both Stacey and Gerard acknowledged something was happening between them, but both were scared. Life circumstances made it difficult for them up to that point. Gerard was traveling and working on documentaries. He and Stacey had to work hard to actually be together in the same geographical location, a place where they could invest time and build a relationship with one another.

So together they started down a new path, in a new direction. They began taking brave and courageous actions toward a future that felt outside of themselves.

*"It seems that we're here to serve—to shine a light on what's happening. We're not creating what's happening. It's already happening without us. We just want people to know about it."*—**Gerard Ungerman**

It was clear to both Gerard and Stacey that they wanted to contribute to the world in a way that was both positive and inspiring.

It started with conversations between them about imagining the world at its best. They shifted their focus on what they wanted to see, instead of looking for everything that was wrong with what they were seeing. It seemed like a small shift, but it made all the difference in outcomes.

Then they considered the many challenges facing humankind, and asked how often they might find disrespect as a major component within nearly every single one of the challenges.

It didn't matter how large or small the conflict, they were able to find some level of disrespect as a component in so many of them: road rage, bullying, environmental degradation, police brutality, and even financial collapse—which they saw as coming about largely due to disrespectful and exploitative practices on the part of the largest financial institutions. Then it "clicked" for them. They asked the big question:

"What if everybody just came to the table with respect as a given?

Where would those problems be?"

They flew directly in the face of what they didn't like and put all their energy into the world they wanted to create. They theorized that if everyone started from a place of respect, many of the world's problems would cease to exist. If they and the world took an agreed upon, authentic sense of respect and infused it into all of the choices we each make—choices that create the problem situations, we would be on our way to resolving them. Once they declared their new direction, they gained clarity about how to move forward. They switched from uncovering lies and pointing out problems—what most of Gerard's work had previously done—and focused on highlighting solutions. They realized there were many great ideas for improving the world. Some people were already implementing those solutions. However, very few people were talking about either the solutions or the people applying them.

For Gerard, whose entire life involved media, it signaled a huge change in direction and opportunity. Both he and Stacey recognized the main media messages were shouting loudly about how the world is falling apart. Messages reinforced why everyone should be afraid, how the world was going to "hell in a hand basket." The underlying message is that it's better to take care of yourself and your family and "throw everybody else to the wolves."

When they stepped back and considered the messages all around them, they realized it just wasn't the way either of them viewed or felt about the world. They see the world as beautiful and amazing, full of people capable of incredible achievements; and that is what they wanted to talk about. So, they changed professional direction.

They started by asking themselves what the best way is to inspire others, and how to meet the people taking action and creating powerful solutions in their own lives.

Gerard began talking through ideas with Stacey. They agreed selling documentaries was difficult. Shooting shorter length films as opposed to feature length made sense. Rather than taking a year and a half or more to complete, a series of shorter videos—two or three minutes long—would be more digestible for people.

Rather than uncovering corruption, lies and deceit, their mission became to seek out and document positive action to inspire change in others. They would tell personal stories about people following their own path, doing things in their unique way. The new format would allow for shorter length videos, promoting hope and inspiring people to action. The videos would be available online, for free.

From making that shift in thinking, *Respectful Revolution* was born in 2012, and established as a national, not-for-profit advocacy organization seeking to document positive action and inspire change.[20]

Gerard and Stacey set out on a journey to learn more about people working in communities across the United States and tell their stories. They decided to profile these local changemakers and introduce them to the rest of the world through short film stories. They decided they would start small in order to create change and "save humanity." Today they are applying their unique skill sets—documentary film making, storytelling, respect, passion and social justice and doing whatever they can to try and influence positive change.

## INSPIRING STORIES

Who inspires and motivates Gerard and Stacey? What types of people impel them to persist in their work?

"Frankly, it's the people whom Stacey and I meet that inspire me. It is uplifting to meet and work with people from all walks of life. Seeing people from all types of backgrounds: social, economic, ethnic, and cultural. People doing all these amazing things, big and small. Seeing this day after day, meeting these people, hearing their stories, and then creating their stories. It fuels the fire that's in me."

When they relate a story about someone that is already making a difference—regardless of scale, and one more person sees that example and either replicates it or goes on to create a slightly different solution, they played the role of changemaker. What if the person they filmed never knew their idea or solution was as powerful until they met and talked about it with Gerard and Stacey? What if through one simple conversation, captured on video, that person got a glimpse of their own greatness and contribution to the world, and as a result ventured further?

## FROM PIG POOP TO POWER

One example is a pig farmer they met last summer in the Midwest. This farmer is what you might call a "MacGyver" of the land. He takes ideas that already exist and tinkers with them to fit his needs.

One thing a pig farmer has an abundance of is pig manure. Lots of it. This farmer decided to build a giant methane gas-trapping bladder in which he put all of the pig manure. He now uses the methane as a power source for his operations. What amazed Gerard and Stacey about this man's invention is that he now runs his entire operation on the fuel that he's trapping from the pig manure. He's not using any grid energy. Best of all, there is no smell because all the manure is in the bladder.

Stacy and Gerard don't know if it's scalable, but they like to think about what might be possible if others who raise animals used his method to capture methane in the same way. Would it allow people living in remote areas to create power for their operations? It might. They do know that people told this farmer he was crazy for investing all his money in something that might not work out. They were inspired that he didn't quit. "He just figured that people get scared and wary of things that they don't know or understand. He also knew and accepted that sometimes things don't work out. But, this time they did."

## WHEN HARD TIMES LEAD TO BETTER OUTCOMES

Another example of what is possible comes through the story of a family ranch just outside Bismarck, ND. This operation is run by a father and son team.

In the mid-nineties the family had to make some hard choices. They had been a traditionally run operation—tilling, using chemical fertilizers and other common practices associated with producing good yields. Four years of drought had taken its toll on the farm. They had smaller yields resulting in less revenue. Fewer resources were available to them to run the farm. They knew they could not afford to keep farming using these practices into the future.

They changed their methods and started regenerative farming. When the crop was harvested they would let the livestock eat the remains rather than tilling. As livestock were in the fields, their manure would provide natural fertilizer for the next crops. These two changes meant more water was retained and the soil was naturally fertilized. They made additional changes as well. Today they farm without tilling; they use only non-GMO seeds and products. The result is they now have a farm that is biodiverse, naturally enriched, with untilled soils that retain moisture and produce healthy, non-GMO foods at a lower cost than other similar operations—and at less than half the cost of chemical farming. What started as financial necessity has turned into a beneficial and profitable operation that produces incredibly good food.[21]


## PASSING HIGH EXPECTATIONS AND VALUES TO THE NEXT GENERATION

It's not only farming and ranching stories that *Respectful Revolution* is spreading. There's the story about Kendric Perkins, a coach and retired Marine and the impact that he is having on a group of kids in New Orleans. Kendric saw a critical need for educating and mentoring youth and his job didn't give him enough time to do it in the way he knew would matter. This was especially true in one part of town where the kids come from very modest, mostly African-American backgrounds. Kendric decided to do something about it. This teacher-coach-mentor took action and started passing on the values and lessons learned from his mom as a young man.

Kendric's mom made sure he had the best education possible so that he could be successful. She wanted him to have opportunities for moving ahead in life. The lessons she taught weren't lost.

The core values and life lessons he shares are embraced by the kids. These lessons would make anyone a better, more conscientious person. But Kendric's kids hold themselves to a higher standard. They know they must uphold and live true to the group's seven core values of: courage, faith, responsibility, wisdom, justice, hope and integrity. They show their commitment by demonstrating: their accountability to others, using 'we' more often than 'I', and taking responsibility for one another.

They take this responsibility seriously and make sure to call each other before a game. It's essential that everyone shows up and no one is left behind. The stakes are high: they only play if everyone is there. Otherwise, they forfeit.

The youth, say that Coach teaches them to "stop kidding around, do your best work, show respect to coaches, adults, and to the park; to help one another and not fight with each other." They know that Kendric cares for his community and is just trying to pass on the lesson he learned from his mom that has helped him succeed.

Kendric believes we should dedicate a good part of our lives to positive mentorship. "Everyone should have something in their heart to give back to their community." Does it have to be as much as Kendric gives? No. But, if everyone gave back to their community, the world would be a better place. And, that could be passed on generation after generation.[22]

# WHAT'S NEXT—ALWAYS REACHING HIGHER

*"After climbing a great hill, one only finds that there are many more hills to climb."*—**Nelson Mandela**

*Respectful Revolution* continues on, only now in a new direction.

Gerard has a greater appreciation for the power of human stories to influence change. The greatest impact comes not so much from the figures and the pie charts generated by data. Those are important and provide one type of understanding. But at the end of the day, it's the personal story that makes the real difference. To share these stories, Gerard and Stacey have been speaking in schools across the country. It's one of the most meaningful ways of bringing encouragement and direction to communities. Students, teachers, and also the administrators tell Gerard and Stacey about the impact of *Respectful Revolution*'s work.

Toward this new future, Stacey and Gerard have launched a new television show. And on April 30, 2016, *Respectful Revolution* had its first national television debut. There is even talk about taking the *Respectful Revolution* message internationally.

Most important, they remain committed to their vision. They ask us to "imagine being able to show the rest of the world the beautiful, generous, respectful side of America; the real America? Yes!!!" They are excited and moving ahead. We are inches away from having our show seen on national TV. We are inches away from being able to find sponsors. And maybe, just maaaaybe, we might have the chance to take this internationally . . . (we're just starting to explore some potentially awesome opportunities.) Imagine being able to show the rest of the world the beautiful, generous, respectful side of America?? The real America? YES!!!

## THE NEXT RIPPLE: INSPIRED BY THOSE WILLING TO STRUGGLE

*"Strength and growth come only through continuous effort and struggle."*—**Napoleon Hill**

While Gerard grew up in France and drew his inspiration initially from films and movies, Stacey's inspiration came from family and nature. Stacey's inspiration remains fueled today by people fighting for social justice; not accepting defeat, even in the face of seemingly overwhelming challenges.

Two people who inspire her most today are Gerard and her aunt.

Gerard for his willingness to invest everything in what they are doing through *Respectful Revolution*, "owning" it all on a very personal level. Even when times are difficult and they don't know how they will pay their bills, Gerard is steady in his commitment.

He works hard—really hard, and is incredibly influential and inspiring to her. "Gerard puts things in perspective, reminding me that our work, *Respectful Revolution*, is not a fluke. It's never felt that way. In fact, as soon as we said "yes" to this new path, we felt the support of the universe." Gerard never lets Stacey forget that.

The other source of inspiration, Stacey's aunt, has had to overcome a lot of tragedy in her life. She was almost killed in a car accident—an accident that took the life of her child, Stacey's young cousin. After the wreck Stacey's aunt could not walk. She was told there was no hope and that her life would always be that way. She rejected all of that rather than accept that she would never walk, would never have children again, would always have back and leg problems. Instead, she healed; she took up running, had two more children, and was voted at age 63 the nation's healthiest woman by Prevention Magazine. Today she runs triathlons. She brings her unwavering strength and knowledge to others as a life coach. She is Stacey's inspiration as she and Gerard push forward.

Four years ago, when *Respectful Revolution* was just getting started, people would question Stacey about why she would go down this new path. They wondered how she and Gerard were going to make a living and survive. It was clear they did not think *Respectful Revolution* would be viable.

But not her aunt. Her aunt never questioned Stacey. Instead, she encouraged Stacey to do whatever it was that seemed to be the right thing to do.

## POSITIVE ACTION IS THE KEY

*"The way to get started is to quit talking and begin doing."*—**Walt Disney**

The trick here is to get out of your head and take positive action. Taking positive action makes things and people better. It's that simple; all you have to do is take the first step.[23]

When you are around folks that understand that positive action is what it takes and they practice that in their lives, we see what is possible.

It doesn't have to be difficult to make a difference. From Gerard and Stacey's perspective, it starts small.

What advice do Gerard and Stacey have for us?

"Just start with a random act of kindness; the simplest thing to do. It's an empowering and freeing thing to do. Just showing consideration for people you don't know. Be polite on the road. Hold a door for somebody. All of these very, very simple things can be done by anybody. It's just that simple. When you are entering a store and open the door for yourself, turn your head, look behind you and see if someone is behind you. Just pause and hold the door for them. Showing kindness to strangers day after day, you will find yourself in a whole new frame of mind. That sets you on a new course that eventually will make you, and everybody around you, happier."

It's these first tiny steps that after a while becomes a regular practice:

**Paying attention, having compassion, caring for the world and others.**

# CHAPTER 7
# CHERIE JAMASON

I met Cherie Jamason more than 20 years ago. We would see each other at meetings of local nonprofit organizations serving children and families. We worked on committees focused on strengthening the nonprofit sector, creating shared visioning and strategies, all for the benefit of improving service delivery throughout our region. Over the years our professional and personal relationship has grown and deepened. Throughout this period my respect and appreciation of her ability to lead by example, ask deep and probing questions, seek better answers, and improve community conditions has grown. She surrounds herself with people who are passionate and capable. She is never satisfied with the status quo. She deliberately learns and grows in order to achieve her goals and lead her organization. It is no surprise then, that among other awards, Cherie was selected after an online national voting process and became the first winner of the national Humanity Inspiration Award in 2014. Her reach truly spans the nation.

## CHERIE'S BACKGROUND

Cherie was born in Connecticut, and although her family moved around quite a bit due to her father's work in sales, she was raised mostly in urban areas of Connecticut and Massachusetts. She considers herself fortunate that her family owned a cottage at Cape Cod, where she not only spent her summers, but her children spent their summers there as well. "Very rustic, and it was the idyllic childhood summer that kids would love to aspire to." For the most part, Cherie reflects on her childhood as being 'very blessed' and the typical three child family, she as the oldest, her middle brother always fighting with their father, and her youngest brother getting away with everything. They seemed to be treated equally, regardless of gender. Cherie's father taught her how to fix lawnmowers, and do plumbing projects; she learned how to cook and do all "that kind of stuff."

Her father instilled in her that she could do anything she wanted, and be anything she aspired to be. Her parents set high standards for her academically, which she always met; because she also had set high standards for herself.

Despite her close-knit family and their openness about their expectations, they shied away from talking about difficult issues, including finances, "They didn't talk about a lot of things that most families should in order to raise normal children." However, her parents were both people of deep faith. Later in life Cherie would need to learn how to deal with and talk about difficult situations and she would find comfort in her faith.

## FROM ONE FAMILY TO ANOTHER

Not long into college, Cherie got married. She had her first two children young as well. Much like her childhood, Cherie moved around a lot with her new husband, as he was transferred every two years or so, "It seemed like I would get pregnant in one state and then have the baby in the next [state], get pregnant in that state and then once again move to a new state, yet again."

As a young mother who moved around a lot, Cherie didn't have the physical support of family, or really any friends to lean on. Then, in 1971 they moved to Canada where they stayed for 15 years. There, they really created a family of their friends and their families. They became involved in the Cursillo[24] movement with its "testimony of friendship and the deepening of the personal conversion" of its members: "We had a lot of friends with families, and those families were friends of one another. They became family for us."

During that time, living in the community, Cherie volunteered with a crisis intervention program that really shaped her desire to contribute to others. At the same time, it gave her an opportunity to go do something that mattered, that gave her an identity other than 'mother'.

## CHALLENGING ROADS AHEAD

*"Roads were made for journeys not destinations."*
—Confucius

For a while, married life was pretty wonderful for Cherie. But in 1979, her husband started exhibiting symptoms of what we now know today as Bipolar Disorder. With little knowledge of the disorder and next to no support during that time, this proved to be a very challenging and painful few years for Cherie. Two more children were added to the family. And, as joyful as that was, being so far from her U.S. family meant these years would take quite a toll on all of them.

They ended up moving to New Hampshire to be closer to their families. They spent another four years in a marriage that they both knew was over. "We went through the separation and divorce routine. Which is never fun."

It was during this time that Cherie became involved with the Hunger Project. It was the beginning of her interest in alleviating hunger. During this time, there was a group of people who would get together on a regular basis that shared an interest in world hunger issues. They ended up raising money to buy a herd of New Hampshire cows for the Heifer Project.[25]

Then, Thanksgiving of 1987 Cherie moved to Reno with three of her children. She needed a job. That's when she became involved with the Food Bank of Northern Nevada (FBNN). The food bank was just five years old and was looking for someone to take it over. Cherie thought, "I could do that!" Not only did she have the skills and enthusiasm to do the job, it was also something very important and close to her heart, "it was kind of a marriage made in heaven."

Cherie reflects:

"I think when I started here [at the Food Bank] I was making about $21,000 a year and had 3 kids and $1,000 a month mortgage. It was very careful budgeting that got me through it, if you will. I just was really grateful that I had the skills that could keep food on the table. We were never behind in payments or anything like that but having a budget was crucial. And being able to cook and put good food on the table for very little money was really important for me at that time. Budgeting and cooking are skills that a lot of the people we serve [through the Food Bank] just don't have. When I think of myself at that time, I realize somebody else might have said we were poor. What I thought of myself and looking at my circumstances, I was 'a middle class person temporarily without money.'"

## A MIDDLE CLASS PERSON TEMPORARILY WITHOUT MONEY

*"Hardships often prepare ordinary people for an extraordinary destiny."*—C. S. Lewis

We know that how we frame our situations makes a huge difference in our lives. Cherie's understanding that she was experiencing a temporary situation that did not define who she was in her own eyes, or in the world, made a significant difference in her ultimate success. "It's a huge distinction because I knew what I needed to do and I had the ability to make a plan and to get myself back on track. I was able to survive with my child support payments and job."

That was a learning period for Cherie, one she would look back on and think, 'what doesn't kill you makes you stronger.' Years later, reflecting back Cherie learned a lot of hard lessons that made her finally able to give up being angry. She was able to realize that all of those experiences made her who she is today.

"I don't know, I thought about it and I'm not the person I used to be, thank God. Living with somebody that's sick like that [with Bipolar Disorder] and that you can't really do anything to help makes you really reliant on your own self. You know that you're the one that has to 'hold it together'. That experience affected me. I didn't do a lot of crying during that time because if I let it go then we would have been in terrible shape." After Cherie and her husband separated, she felt the relief of not having to live under horrible amounts of stress all the time. That made it easier for her to move through life day to day. She also had her work and the value it was adding to the community and her family. Although, there were times that Cherie hid in her work, partly because of necessity being a single mother. As a result, Cherie reflects that this may have been hard on her children, especially the younger ones. Cherie believes the younger kids missed the support she could have given them in school—help that her older kids got.

Through all of the challenges and changes, Cherie took comfort in her spiritual life and liturgical music. Raised a Catholic, she was a canter, a singer and a soloist for 25 years. "Liturgical music was such a part of my life and even today I listen to it and it's beautiful and it brings me a lot of peace. To be able to share that in a way that enriches people is a huge gift and opportunity." Her spiritual life and liturgical music kept her whole and mentally strong.

*"The marvelous richness of human experience would lose something of rewarding joy if there were no limitations to overcome. The hilltop hour would not be half so wonderful if there were no dark valleys to traverse."*
—Helen Keller

## THE FOOD BANK OF NORTHERN NEVADA'S EVOLUTION

*"Once an organization loses its spirit of pioneering and rests on its early work, its progress stops."*
—Thomas J. Watson

What really drove the move from being a food distribution point to direct service were the hunger studies. FBNN was one of the 35 pioneering food banks to participate in the first hunger study in the early '90's. That study showed that two-thirds of the people the FBNN was serving were children and seniors, whereas their partner agencies weren't serving either of those populations.

That was the beginning of the *Kids Café Program*, which started as a summer lunch program in 1991 just because 'it needed to be done.' "If you've got a program that can feed kids in the summertime when school is out and the children rely on us for meals, why wouldn't you do that?"

Once they had some traction with *Kids Café*, the Food Bank started lobbying to get the senior commodity food box program started. It took three years to get the state to put the senior program in the state commodity distribution plan, something which needed to happen before moving forward. But, they finally got it!

FBNN's program changes were driven by data, and if getting food to kids and seniors is what people needed, then Cherie wondered why they wouldn't do that Cherie innately believes that "you've got to do the right thing. If you've got the capacity to do the right thing and you don't do that thing, then shame on you."

And that's how they grew. More and more people were hungry and there wasn't enough food to feed them all. They discovered that they could help people get more food through the *Supplemental Nutrition Assistance Program* (SNAP, formerly food stamps). Nobody else seemed to be doing anything about it at the time. There were thousands more people who were eligible than were using the program. "If we could get them connected with SNAP benefits they could get what they needed. Why wouldn't we do that?"

At the time they were operating out of a 10,000 square foot warehouse that was jammed packed. When one of the neighboring businesses moved, they were able to rent a little more space. They began building a little bit of a financial cushion. They were able to take a second warehouse but still needed a space to call their own to do business—free and clear. That's when Cherie contacted her friend Rodney in Oklahoma that worked with the Reynold's Foundation. The next transformation process began. They received a grant from the Donald W. Reynolds Foundation[26] that caused them to move towards planning, again relying on data. It "upped their game" and the stakes.

Anne Cory is a changemaker in her own right and has known Cherie for more than two decades. Anne has been a human services leader for northern Nevada and the Lake Tahoe Basin, worked with organizations developing permanent supportive housing for people who were homeless in northern California, and is working with the Community Health Alliance in Reno, Nevada. She currently serves on the Steering Committee for the Food Bank's Bridges to a Thriving Nevada initiative.

Anne reflects on the transformation of the Food Bank during this transition period:

"I remember when Cherie first received the Reynolds money and it seemed like she was expecting a fairly straightforward growth, a new building, a bigger facility, more food. The Donald W. Reynolds Foundation does not do things that way. They really demanded total transformation of the organization. Cherie debated whether it was worth it or not, because they were going to become a different organization, there was no doubt."

The Reynolds Foundation was not providing a rigid roadmap, just a very lofty set of expectations. Cherie decided to proceed. There were a lot of ups and downs throughout that process, including the site acquisition and design phase. They had to raise an incredible amount of money on their own; Cherie compromised where she had to, but there were some places where she just stuck to her guns and said, 'No, this is what we need to do.' Then she found people who could help her accomplish those things. "One of the reasons I find that so amazing is that she didn't know how to do any of these things in the beginning. She didn't know capital campaigns. She didn't know buildings. She didn't know site acquisition. And she learned and did all of those things on top of a significant agency transformation; from a pokey little nonprofit to a very streamlined, very innovative organization."

As with many building processes, they were met with obstacles and challenges and heartbreak. With the recession, price of fuel, land issues and transition, it wasn't easy. How did Cherie navigate those challenges? According to Anne: "Cherie's really, really thoughtful about it. She's very self-reflective. She's not always easy on herself, but she definitely thinks it through. She compromises when she needs to, but she decides where she needs to make her stand, and then figures out how to do that. She's both pliable and firm.

When Cherie takes on a challenge, she discusses it frequently with her friends and her trusted advisors, just to check her own perspective."

## THE NATIONAL SCENE

*"The greatest danger for most of us is not that our aim is too high and we miss it, but that it is too low and we reach it."*—**Michelangelo**

Carol Garrity Komen works for Feeding America, which is the national organization of Second Harvest food banks throughout the United States and knows Cherie because FBNN used to be one of the food banks with which Carol worked.

Carol describes Cherie as a big picture thinker who combines vision, heart, and pragmatism:

"She's a very well respected leader. She's a constant voice to concerned citizens in organizations across Nevada on behalf of people struggling with hunger. She is genuine, authentic. She listens very carefully to what you have to say. She has a brilliant mind, which if you know her, you know that. She's very humble."

Carol explains how Cherie is always looking for innovative and efficient solutions and thinking about how she can share those solutions with others. Cherie believes in collaboration and the power of more than just one person or one organization doing the work.

"The biggest thing Cherie brings to the national scene is sharing. She's spoken at many of our conferences and has inspired many to reach further and to do more than they're currently doing."

Cherie has a mind of innovation. She doesn't look at things as barriers or challenges, but she thinks of opportunities and ways she can create innovation to solve some of the problems.

The FBNN is recognized as the expert in hunger issues by the region, the state, and even the national scene. This is because Cherie operates her food bank under the theory of abundance and not scarcity. That has always led her to groundbreaking work. "I really believe that she believes failure is not an option."

First and foremost, Cherie believes in partnership rather than competition. She looks to the community to partner, thereby complimenting each other's work rather than competing. Being in northern Nevada, Cherie didn't always have the resources, yet collaborated with others to either bring those resources in or to create those resources. One example is when she brought in heaps of produce out of California, because they were abundant in California and scarce in Nevada. Yet, she figured out how to work with others to get the healthiest product into Nevada.

Cherie recognizes what is deficient in her area, and then plays the hand of abundance. Therefore she's able to serve her community much better.

"Cherie looks much deeper to find the root of a problem, and teaches others to do the same; that's why she is so well suited for poverty work and her ability to incorporate that into her own organization."

In 2013, FBNN was named Member Food Bank of the year at the Feeding America conference. It was one of over 200 food banks considered. In 2014, Cherie was also presented with the John Van Hengel award for distinguished contributions toward Feeding America's mission to ending hunger in America from Feeding America, which is given by the National Council (a representative group of peer food banks that actually work with Feeding America to align their goals.)

Those are two of the highest national awards, you can receive.

And, in 2010, Cherie was named the 2010 distinguished Nevadan Award. "She's just so humble and quiet, and so well respected that when her name is mentioned the room can be silent. Really, she makes that much of an impression on people."

## ADVICE TO OTHERS

What Cherie would say to others looking to pursue a dream is, "Just go do it, you'll figure it out. Try it, around here we just kind of say, you can try anything for 30 days and if you don't like it, you don't have to do it anymore, but you never know until you try."

"A lot of the stuff that I've done, I had no idea how to do it but if you have that confidence that I gained from my family you can do whatever you set your mind to do. I always believed that whatever it was, I could do it. To have people be able to believe in themselves and just 'have at it' and see what happens is a great gift. If you've got somebody to cheer you on from behind you then all the better."

Cherie believes that the answer is always 'Yes.' If you say no then nothing happens. "Step 1 is 'yes', step 2 is 'I'll figure it out', and step 3 is 'who do I need to talk to find out how?'"

*"Wisdom consists not so much in knowing what to do in the ultimate as knowing what to do next."*
**—Herbert Hoover**

Asking and receiving help is one very important lesson Cherie has learned along the way. She shares that she has a hard time accepting help, as it's easier for her to give. However, Cherie is learning the value in being able to help each other.

Further, Cherie reminds us that "It's about not taking no for an answer. It's the knowledge that we can do this, we know how to do this or we can figure out how to do this. Then it's about being relentless, being persistent." In fact, Anne confirms this sentiment. Anne describes Cherie as someone who is "very inspiring in a very quiet sort of way . . . she thinks big. She always starts with "yes." She does not assume that something *can't* be done. And yet, she's not unrealistic in working through how it can get done."

## WHAT OTHERS HAVE TO SAY ABOUT CHERIE

Laura Dickey has known Cherie Jamason for a number of years. Through Laura's various roles in serving youth, seniors, and providing training came together for her when she applied for a position with the Food Bank of Northern Nevada working with the *Bridges to a Thriving Nevada* initiative and the Getting Ahead Alliance. She considers Cherie a changemaker for her "one step further" approach. No matter what the issue is Cherie seeks to "take it one step further in order to bring people together in partnership and collaboration, to the betterment of the community and the individuals involved." For many people comfortable with traditional food bank operations, the Bridges and Getting Ahead initiatives are not readily linked to ending hunger in their minds. But, Cherie has always seen the potential of community and systems change on individual transformation. Laura tells a story of one man who would not be where he is today, surrounded by a supportive group caring people, without Cherie's foresight and commitment to go beyond feeding people for just one day. Many years ago Cherie introduced the Bridges Out of Poverty work, including the Getting Ahead workshops, to the community as a longer term strategy for ending hunger.

"The Food Bank has been partnering with Volunteers of America, the City of Reno, and Opportunity Alliance since September 2015 to offer the Getting Ahead in a Just Getting by World to residents living in shelters. This particular gentleman was in the first Reno Works group of Getting Ahead students from the men's shelter. Prior to coming to Reno he lived in California. His dream when coming to Reno was to build a new life for himself, his wife and the child they were expecting. He successfully graduated from the program in November 2015, was provided housing through the Rapid Rehousing program and he got a job working as a chef in downtown Reno."

Just as this man was getting his feet under him, his life was nearly taken. In February 2016, he was stabbed outside a local casino. The damage was so severe that he was placed on life support for several days. He was not expected to live or come out of his coma. His wife, only two weeks away from delivering their child, went into early labor because of the stress and worry for her husband. They were both in the hospital at the same time. Throughout their time in the hospital the other Getting Ahead graduates stood by them. Someone was always there.

Miraculously he came out of his coma and started regaining his health.

The baby and wife were both healthy.

Just four weeks after the stabbing he attended another graduating class of Getting Ahead and shared his story. With him were his new born baby, his wife and his mom. "He was in tears. He talked about how Getting Ahead made a difference in his life and how he decided to give back." This is the powerful, transformative work of ending hunger when you think long term results. Other Getting Ahead participants have also had epiphanies. One man told Laura, "Getting Ahead taught me that I could be the man I was meant to be—the man my wife and children deserve." These men now have respect for themselves and their abilities. Getting Ahead helped them become the change in their own lives toward self-sufficiency and prosperity.

Anne shares how Cherie "treats people with incredible respect, always. She truly believes in partnership, and doesn't care who gets the credit. She ensures that others get as much of the credit as she can give to them."

She goes on to say how Cherie "never forgets that she's a mom and grandma. Her family is really important to her. She's overcome a lot of personal challenges without a whole lot of bitterness. And that's just an amazing thing. She acts like it's all so easy but it's hard stuff, and she's really good at it. Yet she's still just 'Cherie' who'd just as soon make supper for you."

Carol also has no shortage of praise for Cherie. She shares: "Cherie always leaves you with exactly what you didn't know you needed. She touches your heart through your head. She's a wonderful, giving individual and she sees the beauty in life and she teaches you how to teach others. She pulls those strings in you that give you the ability to take what she gives you and to give it to others."

Carol goes on to say that Cherie "is one of those people that is put here for a purpose; to impact others. She has all these incredible talents that people admire, but some of the best times is just having a one on one conversation with her."

"Cherie is very well loved, very well respected. She's a national treasure."

## ENDING HUNGER AND THE NEXT GENERATION OF LEADERS

Today Cherie is focused on supporting and growing those with a desire to improve others' lives. It isn't enough for Cherie that she, her staff, board of directors and hundreds of volunteers have grown the organization to what it is today. It isn't even enough that they have made a difference in so many peoples' lives, including those that volunteer and work with the FBNN. She looks ahead at what is left to do: to make sure the work of the past decades is sustained. She sees the need to find and nurture young leaders, to ensure they have a place at the table, and that they are included in decision-making. These new leaders need support as they assume responsibilities for directing resources, making policy, and partnering in solutions that change the landscape for those living in poverty.

## WHO INFLUENCED CHERIE

"I think my dad was the biggest influence on me. It's interesting, it just chokes me up and he's been gone for 15 years."

Cherie's father never really shared much about his military service experience. It wasn't until much later in life she learned that one of his roles during the war was receiving returning prisoners of war, feeding them and helping them to regain their health.

And then, when he was in his 70's, as part of their church, he would cook meals and bring them to the missions in Los Angeles. That really affected Cherie's father, meeting the people that would come in to the missions. He told Cherie about one young man who came in barefoot in the middle of winter because someone stole them while he slept. That experienced moved Cherie's father so deeply that he began to see people differently.

"I always wanted him to be proud of me and I think he was. Especially later in life when the Food Bank got bigger and bigger, he was just incredibly proud. He was so proud of the work that we do here and of my part in it. It was a joy to be able to talk about that and get ideas from him. Of all the people in my life who most hugely influenced me, I think it would be my dad."

## LEGACY OF HELPING

*"Help your brother's boat across, and your own will reach the shore."*—**Hindu Proverb**

Not only was Cherie's father a 'helper' like Cherie, so too are her daughters. That's three generations—a legacy—of helping.

"Nancy works for food [she owns a well-known restaurant famous for upscale comfort food, using fresh organic ingredients to create fun, festive, flavorful dishes] and she just idolized her grandfather. Katie with her yoga, is helping people in their health. My older daughter Tracy is a writer of Christian books and her life really is greatly about helping families in her own way. Now that her children are both in college she volunteers with her community's assistance league and the senior residential program. That just blows my mind. She and my mom were very close. She volunteers more now with her kids gone. She saw that was what my parents did, that's the kind work that I do, that's what she's doing. It's very cool."

# CHAPTER 8
# WHAT DISTINGUISHES THESE SIX INDIVIDUALS AS CHANGEMAKERS?

Throughout this book these six changemakers shared with us their lessons and tips for success. There were several mutual characteristics among and between these individuals. However, there are ten specific qualities that they all share, and are pivotal to their success and impact on others.

## 1. LEADERSHIP

First and foremost, everyone you just read about is a leader. Whether they were born leaders, or developed their leadership abilities along the way, it is deeply engrained in all of them. Take Michelle for example. Everyone she came into contact with looked up to her and looked to her for advice. They saw her as a strong leader whom could help steer them in the right direction. Michelle is infectious and people want to be around her. That's what a good leader does.

It takes a special kind of person to be a true leader—someone that others look up to and want to follow; some might say that this kind of special can't be taught. Think about how Cherie was able to build a large, streamlined and innovative organization, all from a small non-profit; you can't do that alone. The way she was able to get people to buy into her vision, to do things to make it happen—they did it because they believed in her; in her dream—that's not an easy feat!

## 2. INITIATIVE

The difference between someone that succeeds and everyone else, is when a changemaker has a dream or goal and they encounter a problem, they continue ahead. Instead of complaining about the situation or looking for someone else to fix it, they are the ones who take initiative and instinctively want to resolve it. You can see this throughout Ian's entire story. Every problem that Ian encountered, he immediately stepped in to fix it. From the girls soccer team, to taking them to see the Women's World Cup in Canada, to a lack of programming for kids and creating programs where there weren't any—he was a leader who took action; he made things happen, a real changemaker. When Julian faced technical difficulties during the record attempt, he stepped up and found a workable solution. And, faced with a knee injury, Michelle's response was to take care of herself and heal, at the same time she looked for ways to continue her training goals.

## 3. MOTIVATING OTHERS

Motivation is exactly how these changemakers are able to cause a ripple effect. Having buy-in from others is one thing, but mobilizing them to make things happen, to create real change—that's on a whole other level. Every one of these changemakers connect with people about what matters to them; they look at the world and see possibility and how they can share that with others. Ian was on the right track with this one. His simple but ground-breaking approach of providing volunteers with a meaningful experience that fit their comfort level and interests, rather than what the organization 'needs' is integral to how he was able to mobilize others to realize his vision.

Speaking of the ability to mobilize others, no one quite did this like Julian. The way Julian was able to get over 900 musicians, countless volunteers, and a regular audience to work around the clock for almost 35 days straight is nothing short of brilliant. This is when real change not only happens, but ripples outward to create further change. This is evident in Julian's second Guinness attempt as well as his additional projects—people were in before he even had to ask!

## 4. HELP AND GUIDANCE

All of the individuals asked for and accepted help and guidance. No one believed they could or should do it all on their own. Throughout her life Michelle has learned from others how to accomplish certain goals. Whether piloting a yacht, getting a youth back on track, or learning how to heal from injury or address Multiple Sclerosis, she asks questions and obtains support. From the start, Ian sought support from non-profit and community leaders to help him build out his vision in Reno. He continued to ask for help and support as he expanded his work to Canada and Africa. Julian conducted extensive research and then asked for expert help in promoting and marketing his event. It took hundreds of community volunteer hours to pull it off and document results. Gerard and Stacey found help and guidance in one another. They connected with others in the community change movement to receive support. To this day, Cherie continues to seek expert advice and guidance in the fields of collective impact, organizational change and community leadership.

## 5. PASSION

However, none of this would be possible without true passion on the part of the changemaker. Undoubtedly, Ian, Julian, Michelle, Stacey, Gerard and Cherie all share this trait. Passion is what drives them in their endeavors; it's what picks them up when they fall down; it's what gets them over the hurdles and obstacles thrown in their way. Most people would've given up at the first sign of failure or when their efforts seemed futile; but that's where these six changemakers differ from most people. Without passion, there would be no Respectful Revolution, no Let Them Be Kids, no Food Bank of Northern Nevada (or at least what it is today), no I Play in Chico, and no Humankind. Be Both®. All of this was born out of passion, grew out of passion, and continues to grow from the passion of these six incredible individuals.

## 6. DETERMINATION

While many people are passionate about many things, if they aren't determined, their dreams will fall flat. So, not only are these six individuals passionate about their cause(s), they show incredible determination to succeed. Determination can present itself in something as simple as not taking no for an answer or writing a letter of request every day for one year. But, these changemakers all share the deepest kind of determination: *perseverance in the face of adversity.* This is where the age old question of which came first (the chicken or the egg) might appear. Almost everyone we read about faced great adversity at a very young age: Ian's rough upbringing; Julian's experiences with being severely bullied; and, Gerard's absence of a father figure and caring mother. And, some later in life with Cherie's marriage and divorce, and Stacey's great empathy for her Aunt's tragic loss. Did these experiences shape who they are today? Are their experiences and upbringing the reason why they are so strong and determined today? Have these experiences shaped their response to adversity? Or, would they be the same person despite their adversity? Whatever the answer, it is evident that all of these changemakers are stronger than the average person, more determined than most, and persevere where others would quit.

## 7. COMMITMENT

Which, brings us to our next common characteristic: commitment. It is safe to say that each of these individuals is committed to their goals and passions. Nothing shows commitment like rushing through 12 long city blocks with 60 pounds of evidence and luggage to reach Guinness on time, or not taking something at face value and delving deeper to determine the real reason a child isn't attending school regularly. Commitment is giving everything up to reconnect with your true self and to nature, and it's donating all of your supplementary income so kids can just be kids.

# 8. PURPOSE

Another quality these individuals all have in common is that they all have a very strong sense of purpose, a purpose higher than themselves. They each work from a grassroots mindset. Ian, with LTBK, his community soccer leagues, The Changing Point, and Becoming a Community Leader, you really can't get any more grassroots and community focused than that. And, creating a sense of community from the grassroots level is exactly what Julian intended to do—to drive community growth and purpose in the local music scene—through I Play in Chico and going for Guinness. Michelle's sense of purpose and community even shows in her personal life when she lived in DC and Lake Tahoe, becoming a Deacon and an Elder, and serving as Board President of the Homeowners Association. She continues that with her expanded community in Humankind. Be Both.® When Stacey and Gerard began Respectful Revolution, they really wanted to focus on others' purpose by revealing the positive things that were happening in their community, and then communities across the U.S. They work so as many people as possible can know about what is possible and make changes in their own communities. And, no matter what Cherie takes on, she is particularly skilled in bringing people together for the betterment of the community.

## 9. INNOVATION

All of these changemakers are also highly innovative and inspired to do things that had never been done before, or done in a particular way in a particular community. For Gerard and Stacey to make such a drastic shift from exposing horrors and corruption to *Respectful Revolution*—an innovative and exhilarating change, despite criticism from others—took real courage and inspiration. Almost all of Ian's endeavors had never been done before, especially *Let Them Be Kids* in Canada; and of course, Julian's record attempt for the longest concert had been done before, but the target goal had never been *double* that of the current record, nor done as inclusively. All of these changemakers looked for gaps that needed to be filled and they were moved to create change that would be innovative, long-lasting and cause a ripple effect.

## 10. START SMALL

Finally, each and every person we just read about started small; they truly believe that just one person can make a difference—and, they all showed us that it's possible. Ian explains that what he did happened because he started small and his advice to others is to do the same: "If everyone just handles their own little corner of the world, the plain and simple fact is, we'd have a better world." Michelle may have viewed her impact on people like Joe, Maurice, Alan, Sarah, Jon,

Marian, Armando and Bonnie to be quite insignificant but that couldn't be further from the truth. Michelle was just being herself with these individuals, but the impact was larger than life and as a result, all of her care, attention and love rippled outward. The videos that Gerard and Stacey now make are short and available for free; and, the impact is greater than they could've ever imagined. Three decades ago Cherie began working with three people from a 4,000 square foot warehouse, serving a local community. Today there are nearly 60 employees working out of 70,000 square feet in order to handle the demand throughout Northern Nevada and eight California counties.

Each of these incredible individuals is passionate and knew what they wanted. They went "all in," even when they didn't know what exactly that would entail. They were each willing to risk, go outside of their comfort zones and trust in themselves, even when the way forward was not immediately clear. They took bold action at whatever level was necessary; and when met with challenges or obstacles, they persevered. They were humble enough to ask for help when they needed it and they studied, asked questions and were curious to learn what they needed to know to move forward. All along the way, they learned, grew and adapted to change.

None of them consider themselves perfect, or finished. Each knows that you succeed because you are standing on the shoulders of others who have gone before so that you can reach a hand back to those who want to follow next. All are willing to share what they know and have learned with others.

There is no failure, only experience.


## NOW IT'S YOUR TURN

If you've made it this far in the book, it's likely you are someone who is already "out there" making a difference. Perhaps, like many of us with a dream of improving our "corners of the world," you are someone who sees yourself as an "everyday hero," just waiting for your time; your chance to make a difference. Or, maybe you are waiting for someone to invite you to take action.

This is your invitation. Your time is now. Don't rob the world of your contribution just because you are not certain of the path forward. Take cues from the stories in this book and map your course—even just the first few steps. Ask for support and guidance when and where you need it. Accept help when offered, and remember the best way to achieve something is to move in the direction of your goal. Your steps forward can be small, but you must persist in taking them.

Thank you for buying this book, whether for yourself, or for friends, family, co-workers or colleagues. Or because you want to help end hunger.

Thank you changemakers, all.

# ENDNOTES

1. Food Bank of Northern Nevada, www.fbnn.org

2. Seneca, http://en.wikiquote.org/wiki/Seneca_the_Younger

3. Goodreads, www.goodreads.com/quotes/17490-luck-is-what-happens-when-preparation-meets-opportunity

4. Booker T. Washington, www.booker-t-washington.com/booker_t_washington.htm

5. PBS, www.pbs.org/wnet/jimcrow/stories_people_booker.html

6. Carson Now, www.carsonnow.org/story/01/26/2016/director-returns-brewery-arts-center-carson-city-where-dance-career-began

7. Becoming a Community Builder, www.becomingacommunitybuilder.com/index.php/alberta

8. Owned by Kraft Foods

9. www.facebook.com/Let-Them-Be-Kids-154051810186/

10. Filmed by Get Foxy Productions

11. I Play in Chico, www.youtube.com/watch?v=QMQOa7LFTRA/

12. Joyful Days, www.joyfuldays.com/trust-in-god-but-tie-up-your-camel/

13. Julian Ruck, www.facebook.com/julian.ruck

14. Look to the Stars, www.looktothestars.org/celebrity/jackson-browne

15. Jake Shimabukuro, www.jakeshimabukuro.com

16. Broadway World, www.broadwayworld.com/bwwmusic/article/NVOH-Presents-Ukulele-Legend-Jake-Shimabukuro-319-20100309

17. A 1990 movie starring Christian Slater

18. Brainy Quote, www.brainyquote.com/search_results.html?q=challenges&pg=3

19. A three-part mini-series about the CIA

20. Learn more at www.RespectfulRevolution.org

21. Respectful Revolution, www.respectfulrevolution.org/road/videos/gabe_paul_brown_regenerative_ranching

22. Respectful Revolution, www.respectfulrevolution.org/road/videos/kendric_perkins_kids_wisner

23. Barton Goldsmith, Ph.D. (*Psychology Today*, January 7, 2014)

24. Cursillo Movement of Canada, www.cursillos.ca/en/cursillo.htm

25. Heifer International, www.heifer.org/

26. Donald W. Reynolds Foundation, www.dwreynolds.org

# ABOUT THE AUTHOR

If it's a little scary, makes her stretch, challenges self-perceived limitations, and offers a chance to grow and partner with others, Sarah Boxx is all in. If she can help connect someone with a dream or goal, she's thrilled. Sarah knows what it is to start down a path where she might not succeed, yet does so knowing where and how to garner support and inspiration from people and life's experiences. Sarah has always trusted her "gut" and instincts about the need for change, even when she didn't know the path forward or how it opened to the future.

Today Sarah is a partner at a boutique consulting firm dedicated to improving the lives of people by helping organizations realize their potential through building the skills, knowledge and experiences to plan and achieve their visions. Each year she coaches a select number of high achievers who have passion and determination to accomplish their goals. Not limited to traditional ways of thinking, she combines her analytical and creative skills to help people assess quickly what matters most to them and then chart a clear path from dreaming into achieving.

If you want to know more about Sarah Boxx and her work as coach and consultant, visit her at www.sarahboxx.com and www.socialent.com.

Made in the USA
Middletown, DE
09 October 2016